Acknowledgements

The Scottish Consumer Council is indebted to Shelley Gray for producing the majority of the text for this handbook.

We would also like to extend our thanks to the many people and organisations who commented on drafts of the handbook. All their comments helped make this handbook stronger and more accurate. In particular we would like to thank:

• Gareth Allen, Office of the President of the Additional Support Needs Tribunals for Scotland

• Tam Baillie, Barnardo's Scotland

• Eric Drake, Scottish Public Services Ombudsman

• Linda Dunion, 'see me' campaign

• Eddie Follan, Children in Scotland

• Miranda Harvey, Scottish Parent Teacher Council

• Jenny Hill, Child Brain Injury Trust

• Sue Ross, Tourette Scotland

• Mhairi Snowden, Skill Scotland

• Margaret Sutherland, Scottish Network for Able Pupils

Administrative support for this project was provided by Susan Collie and Lorraine Urie at the Scottish Consumer Council.

Contents

Part 1:
Introduction

1.1 What is this handbook for?

Many children and young people need extra help at some point while they are at nursery or school. This might be because of a short term issue or could be related to ongoing circumstances. There is a new system in place for supporting your child and this handbook aims to guide you through that system. The Education (Additional Support for Learning) (Scotland) Act 2004 (called the Additional Support for Learning Act for the remainder of this handbook) replaces the system for 'Special Educational Needs'. The Act came into effect in November 2005 and applies to all children who need extra support, not just those with disabilities or recognised medical conditions.

In addition to this handbook, you can get information and advice from Enquire which is the Scottish advice and information service for additional support for learning. The service is run by Children in Scotland and funded by the Scottish Executive and it can give you advice and information through its telephone helpline, website and wide range of free publications (see section 7.6 for contact details). This handbook will give you general information about the additional support needs system but if you have questions about your individual situation that it cannot answer we recommend that you get in touch with Enquire.

You can also contact your education authority for information (including information that is specific to your local area). The law says that your education authority must have a named person who can provide you with information and advice if your child has additional support needs. You can find out who this is either by asking a member of staff at your child's school/nursery or by contacting the education department of your local council. For the rest of this handbook we will call this the 'education authority contact person'.

1.2 How to use this handbook

We have structured the handbook to lead you through the system:

- Part 1: Introduction gives you background information about the additional support needs system as well as an at a glance guide to you and your child's rights and responsibilities.

- Part 2: Additional Support Needs focuses on what we mean by 'additional support needs' including how you can find out whether or not your child needs additional support and how their needs will be assessed.

- Part 3: Providing Additional Support outlines what happens if your child has additional support needs, including provision that can be made by the school and other agencies. There is also a section on how the school will plan for your child's additional support needs (including the co-ordinated support plan).

- Part 4: Stages of schooling gives information on what happens when your child starts or moves school, and what happens when they are planning to leave school. There is also a section here on home education.

- Part 5: Being involved and dealing with problems talks you through the complaints mechanisms available, including mediation, dispute resolution and the role of the Additional Support Needs Tribunals.

- Part 6: Other issues gives you information about more general issues which may affect your child.

- Part 7: Reference section includes a range of useful information including a glossary of terms and professionals, a description of common situations that might lead to additional support needs, a comprehensive reading list for further information, and an overview of other sources of assistance.

> We hope that parents will be able to dip in and out of the sections that are relevant to them without needing to read the handbook all at once.

This handbook explains your rights under the new legislation but it does not give a full explanation of the law on education and should not be taken as the 'last word' in the law. Only the courts can decide exactly how the law should be interpreted and while every effort has been taken to ensure that this handbook is accurate and up-to-date, you should take advice about any further changes to the law since it was published. Part 5 provides a list of contacts; here you will find many sources of advice and information on additional support needs. The Scottish Consumer Council regrets that it cannot itself deal with individual enquiries.

We have used a number of legal terms throughout this handbook. Most are explained in the glossary at the end. However the words 'should' and 'must' are often used in relation to the legal obligations of education authorities. Where we use 'must' this means that the education authority has a legal requirement to do something. On the other hand, when we use 'should' this means that Scottish Executive guidance says that it would be good practice for the authority to do so.

Definition of parent

In education law, the term parent includes:

• a guardian
• anyone who has parental responsibility for a child
• anyone who has a duty to pay maintenance for a child
• anyone who has day to day control of a child.

1.3 How does this handbook relate to the Additional Support for Learning Code of Practice?

The Scottish Executive has published a Code of Practice on the Additional Support for Learning Act (called Supporting Children's

Learning). This is meant to give guidance to those who work in the additional support for learning system, particularly school and social work staff and health professionals. The Code of Practice has some legal weight as education authorities and other agencies such as health boards and social work departments must 'have regard' to what it says.

Some of the information in this book comes from the Code of Practice and where we have directly copied information this has been clearly marked. You can view the Code of Practice on the internet at www.ltscotland.org.uk or you may be able to get a copy from the Scottish Executive Education Department. Each school in Scotland has been sent a copy so you can ask your child's teacher or nursery manager if you can see theirs. You can also ask the additional support for learning contact person (see section 5.2) in the education authority to let you see a copy.

1.4 Background – policy and legislation

Definition of additional support needs

Your child has additional support needs if they need extra support (compared with their classmates) to get the most out of school and achieve their full potential. This does not just mean doing well academically but also applies if they need help with other aspects of school. For example they might need support with social skills and developing confidence or help with extra-curricular activities.

The term 'additional support needs' covers a wide range of situations that might mean a child needs extra support. For example it includes long term needs such as an ongoing disability or health issue as well as temporary difficulties such as family breakdown (where this affects a child's education). The term could also apply to your child if they are particularly able and need a specialised approach to help them reach their full potential (page 12 gives a fuller explanation of the definition of additional support needs).

The Additional Support for Learning Act replaced the previous system (often called the Record of Needs system) that was introduced by the Education (Scotland) Act 1980. This system used the term Special Educational Needs (SEN) and applied to a far smaller number of children and young people with a narrower range of needs. The decision to review the Record of Needs system was made as a result of the recommendations of the Riddell Report in 1999 (Report into the education of children with severe low incidence disabilities) which highlighted many problems experienced by children, young people, parents and professionals. The Scottish Executive carried out the review (called Assessing our children's educational needs: the way forward?) between 2001 and 2002 and asked parents, professionals and children and young people what they thought of the Record of Needs system and what should be done to improve it. The conclusion was that there should be a more inclusive system with more rights for parents and greater consistency across the country in the way children and young people's needs are met. After further consultation on what the new system should look like, the Additional Support for Learning Act was passed by the Scottish Parliament and came into force in November 2005. This replaced entirely the Record of Needs system.

The decisions to carry out an inquiry into SEN and then to review the system were part of wider moves towards greater equality and inclusiveness. In 1991 the UK adopted the United Nations Convention on the Rights of the Child (UNCRC) that emphasises the rights of disabled children to the support they need to lead a full, independent and included life. This was strengthened in 1994 when the United Nations Education, Social and Cultural Organisation (UNESCO) produced the Salamanca Statement that recommended that all countries introduce inclusive education for disabled children.

In Scotland there have been a number of key developments in the move towards inclusion and high quality services for disabled people. In 1999 (in the Beattie Report Implementing Inclusiveness: Realising Potential) the Scottish Executive agreed that all post-school education should be based on the principle of inclusion and in 2000 the Scottish Executive published Same as you?, a report that introduced policies meant to improve the lives and level of inclusion of people with learning disabilities. One of the most significant pieces of legislation was the Standards in Scotland's Schools etc. Act 2000. This introduced new rights for children and parents to be involved in decision-making in education and brought in the presumption that all children should be educated in mainstream schools wherever possible. This was followed in 2002 by the introduction of a requirement on local authorities to produce accessibility strategies outlining how they will improve access to education for disabled pupils. These developments build on the UK-wide Disability Discrimination Act (DDA) 1995 which makes it illegal for an education authority or public service provider to discriminate against disabled people. At the time of writing government plans were in place to extend the DDA to require public bodies (for example local councils) to promote equality for disabled people.

The Additional Support for Learning Act is meant to deliver a Scottish education system that is inclusive for all children and young people. It is based on the view that it is not the job of a child with an additional support need to change to fit their nursery or school, but rather that the environment must adapt to meet the needs of the child. The Act was also an attempt to move away from labelling particular children as having SEN and instead emphasising that any child or young person might need extra support at some time during their education.

1.5 Key legislation at a glance

Disability Discrimination Act 2005

- Requires public bodies to promote equality of opportunity for disabled people

Education (Disability Strategies and Pupils' Educational Records (Scotland)) Act 2002 (see section 6.1)

- Requires local authorities to write and implement accessibility strategies every three years

Standards in Scotland's Schools etc. Act 2000

- Gives all children of school age the right to education
- Requires education authorities to take account of the views of children and young people in decisions that significantly affect them
- Gives children the right to appeal against school exclusions
- Requires education authorities to provide education in a mainstream school except where particular circumstances apply (see section 6.4)

Adults with Incapacity (Scotland) Act 2000

- Allows for decisions to be made on behalf of people 16 years and over who are not able to make decisions themselves either because of 'mental disorder' or the inability to communicate

Race Relations (Amendment) Act 2000

- Requires public bodies (including schools) to eradicate racial discrimination and promote equality and good race relations

Human Rights Act 1998

- Gives legal weight to the European Convention on Human Rights in Scotland and supports the requirement on public bodies (including local authorities) not to discriminate on any grounds

Disability Discrimination Act 1995 (Part 4) (see section 6.1)

- Makes it illegal for an education authority to discriminate against disabled pupils, requires education authorities to make sure that disabled pupils are not treated less favourably and make 'reasonable adjustments' to avoid putting disabled pupils at a disadvantage

Children (Scotland) Act 1995

- Requires local authorities to safeguard and promote the interests of children in need (this includes disabled children)
- Requires local authority services to be designed to minimise the effect on children of their own, or a family member's, disability and to give them the opportunity to lead as normal a life as possible

Further and Higher Education (Scotland) Act 1992

- Requires that there must be adequate and efficient provision of further and higher education in Scotland
- States that particular consideration must be given to the needs of young people with a disability that may affect their education

Age of Legal Capacity Act 1991 (see section 1.7)

- Gives particular rights (e.g. to instruct a solicitor in civil proceedings and to consent to / refuse medical treatment) to children with capacity (having capacity means they understand the decisions they are making).

1.6 Overview of your rights and responsibilities

As a parent you have particular rights and responsibilities in relation to your child receiving extra support at school.

You have the right to:

- Ask the education authority to find out whether or not your child has additional support needs (section 2.4)

- Ask the education authority to assess whether or not your child needs a co-ordinated support plan (CSP) (section 2.4)
- Ask the education authority to carry out a review of your child's co-ordinated support plan (CSP) (section 3.5)
- Request a particular type of assessment (section 2.4)
- Use independent mediation services (section 5.7)
- Make a placing request asking that your child goes to an independent grant-aided special school (section 4.4)
- Be told the outcome of any request (e.g. for an assessment, review, etc) and be given information on the appeal options open to you
- Receive information and advice about your child's additional support needs and a copy of their CSP if they have one
- Appeal to an Additional Support Needs Tribunal (almost solely for issues relating to CSPs) (section 5.10)
- Use the Dispute Resolution process for issues that cannot be taken to the Additional Support Needs Tribunal (section 5.9)
- Take a supporter or representative (this can be an advocate) with you to any meeting with the school or education authority and to the Additional Support Needs Tribunal (section 5.6)
- See any information the school or education authority has about your child (section 5.2)
- Educate your child at home (the law says you must ask permission to take your child out of school but you do not have to do this if your child has never gone to a local authority school) (section 4.6)
- Appeal against the exclusion of your child from school
- Comment on school plans (e.g. the School Development Plan, local authority's Statement of Improvement Objectives and Accessibility Strategy) (section 5.4).

You have the responsibility to:

- Ensure your child (if they are of school age, approximately 5 to 16) receives education that is appropriate for their age, ability and aptitude

- Safeguard your child's health, development and welfare
- Provide direction and guidance to your child in a way that is suitable for their age
- Maintain regular direct contact and personal relations with your child if they are not living with you
- Act as your child's legal representative.

1.7 Your child's rights

If your child is aged 16 or over they can do all of the above on their own behalf. If your child is under 16 they have the right to:

- Receive school education (see section 4.3)
- Be involved in decisions that affect them (including planning their own education and decisions about the school more generally) (see section 5.5)
- Comment on school plans (e.g. the School Development Plan, local authority's Statement of Improvement Objectives and Accessibility Strategy) (see section 5.5)
- Appeal against decisions to exclude them from school (section 6.3)
- Not be discriminated against if they are disabled (section 6.1)
- Refuse or give consent to medical treatment (if they have legal capacity – see box).

Definition of legal capacity

Certain rights and responsibilities are dependent upon a person having legal capacity. This means that the person has sufficient understanding about the decision they are making and the implications of it. Children are presumed to have legal capacity from the age of 12 but a younger child may have an adequate level of understanding in which case they would have legal capacity. Equally a child over the age of 12, and indeed over 16, may lack capacity.

Decisions about whether or not your child has capacity will be taken by the relevant professional in discussion with you (for example a medical professional would decide if your child had capacity to consent to, or refuse, medical treatment).

United Nations Convention on the Rights of the Child (UNCRC)

A lot of Scotland's education law is based on the UNCRC. This is an international agreement that has been signed by almost every country in the world (signed by the UK in 1991). It gives children a range of rights including: the right to express views and have these taken into account in decisions that affect them; and the right of disabled children to have access to services including education, health care and recreation opportunities.

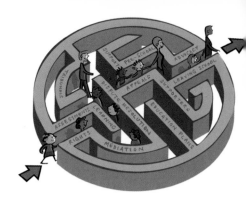

Part 2:
Additional support needs

2.1 What are additional support needs?

If your child has additional support needs it means that they need extra support (compared with their classmates) to get the most out of school. The way the law describes this is to say that your child needs extra support to 'benefit from school education'. The phrase 'school education' has a legal meaning that describes what the purpose of education should be. This says that school education is not just about enabling your child to do well academically but that it must also give them the opportunity to develop personally and help them to achieve their full potential.

Definition of school education

The Education (Scotland) Act 1980 defines school education as: progressive education appropriate to the requirements of pupils in attendance at schools, regard being had to the age, ability and aptitude of such pupils.

This definition was extended by the Standards in Scotland's Schools etc. Act 2000 which says that education authorities must make sure that education is: directed to the development of the personality, talents and mental and physical abilities of the child or young person to their fullest potential.

This recognises that education is not just about academic achievement but that it must also address your child's wider learning needs.

The Additional Support for Learning Act Code of Practice gives more details on what is meant by your child being able to 'benefit from school education'. It lists what all children need to be able to benefit from school education and says that if there is a difficulty in one or more of these areas then this might lead to your child having additional support needs.

> **Definition of benefit from school education**
>
> To be able to benefit from school education you child needs to:
>
> - Be taught in a way which supports their learning and personal development
> - Receive teaching and support which meets their needs
> - Be able to learn with and from their peers
> - Have their learning supported at home and in their wider community.

Here are a few examples of situations which might lead to your child having additional support needs:

- Difficulties with family circumstances – e.g. family breakdown or where your child is a young carer or a young parent
- Disability or health issues – e.g. if your child has a sensory impairment, learning difficulties, or a complex disability
- Problems with the learning environment – e.g. if your child is gifted and is not being challenged by their classes or if English is their second language
- Children in need of care and protection – e.g. if your child has supervision requirements put in place by a children's hearing
- Social and emotional issues – e.g. if your child is being bullied or has behavioural difficulties.

These are just a few examples of situations that could mean your child needs extra support. It is important to remember that the way in which something affects one child can be very different from how it affects another. For example if your child lost a relative they might need a lot of ongoing support as a result whereas another child in their class might have a similar experience and need very little support – it is the effect on your child's individual needs that is important and that is what should dictate the support your child gets (for more on types of situations that might lead to additional support needs see section 7.2).

2.2 What are complex and multiple support needs?

Your child might have additional support needs that have only a small impact on their ability to get the most out of education. They might need extra help in just one area of learning, for example extra help with spelling or with a particular subject. However if your child is in a situation or has a condition that has a significant adverse effect on their education then their support needs would be said to be complex.

There is not a precise definition of complex needs or of how much your child's learning has to be affected before their needs would be considered to have a 'significant adverse effect'. Generally though, your child has complex support needs if they need a high level of support and if most areas of their learning are affected.

Your child might also have a range of needs which individually are not complex, but combined have a significant adverse effect. In law this means they have 'multiple needs'.

If your child has complex or multiple needs they might require a co-ordinated support plan (CSP) (see section 3.4). The decision about whether your child has complex or multiple needs will be taken by the education authority on the basis of assessment (section 2.4).

For more on types of situations that might lead to additional support needs see section 7.2.

Case studies

Here are some examples of the kinds of situations which might lead to your child having complex or multiple support needs:

Louise is in Primary 7 and is experiencing difficult circumstances at home because of parental alcohol problems and domestic abuse. This makes it very hard for her to concentrate in class or to do homework. Louise has also started to truant from school.

Ashok is in his first year of secondary school. He has cerebral palsy and does not communicate verbally. Ashok needs day to day assistance with personal care needs and teaching methods adapted to suit his communication needs.

Peter has mild hearing difficulties and behavioural problems. Neither problem alone causes significant difficulty but put together they make it difficult for him to settle in to his nursery school.

Gail is in fourth year of secondary school and has depression. She has periods of time where she needs little support but at other times she finds it very difficult to go to school and keep up with her work and she needs support to cope.

Sally is in third year of secondary school and helps to care for her dad who is seriously ill. Looking after her dad takes up a lot of her time and means that she is often very tired in class, regularly misses school and finds the situation emotionally difficult.

2.3 What happens if my child has a Record of Needs?

If your child is already in education they may have a Record of Needs from the old Special Educational Needs system. This part of the handbook explains what will happen if your child has a Record of Needs. There are important differences between the Record of Needs system and the new Additional Support for

Learning system. Before reading this section of the handbook it may be helpful to read the section which explains the criteria for a co-ordinated support plan (CSP) being prepared (section 3.4).

If your child has a Record of Needs he/she will not automatically have a CSP prepared. This is because the CSP is not a direct replacement for the Record of Needs and the criteria for preparing (i.e. opening) one is different (see section 3.4). However, regardless of whether your child has a CSP the education authority must by law provide them with the additional support they need.

If your child has a Record of Needs the education authority will assume that they have additional support needs. However the authority will not assume that your child needs a CSP and this will have to be assessed. The education authority must assess whether or not your child needs a CSP by 14th November 2007 (which is two years after the Additional Support for Learning Act came into force).

If your child has a Record of Needs the school should give you information about when they expect to carry out a CSP assessment. If you are not given this information you can ask your child's school or contact the additional support for learning contact person within the education authority (see section 5.2).

Safeguards to your child's support

The law says that until your child is assessed for a CSP the education authority cannot reduce the support they receive unless their needs change significantly and this leads to a change in their support. If your child has a Record of Needs, the only situations where their support could be changed before 14th November 2007 would be if:

• The education authority carries out an assessment and establishes that your child needs a CSP (see section 2.4)

• Your child's needs change significantly.

If the authority assesses your child to see whether they need a CSP there are two possible outcomes:

- The authority finds that your child does need a CSP in which case a CSP must be prepared and the support your child is given would be decided and agreed on through the usual CSP process (see section 3.5). This support will not necessarily be the same as was in your child's Record of Needs
- The authority finds that your child does not need a CSP in which case the support your child receives must not be reduced for the following 2 years (unless their needs change significantly).

If your child is assessed to see if they need a CSP and you do not agree with the outcome you can appeal to the Additional Support Needs Tribunal (see section 5.10).

Case studies

Ling is in her first year of secondary school and has had a Record of Need since she was in primary 3. Her school contacts her parents in summer 2006 to say that they plan to assess her for a CSP. The assessment is carried out and the decision is made that, although Ling has complex needs, she does not need a CSP as all the support she requires will come from within the education department. The law says that the support Ling receives must not be reduced for the next 2 years unless there is a significant change in her needs. The law also says that Ling's additional support needs must be met as long as she is in school education.

Joe is in primary 7 and has had a Record of Need since he started school. His school carries out an assessment to see whether he needs a CSP and decides that one should be prepared. A CSP meeting is arranged to decide what support Joe should be given. This involves discussing what learning outcomes Joe should be achieving over the next year and deciding what support he will need to do this. The CSP is agreed and some of the support from the Record of Need is continued while some is changed.

2.4 How do I find out whether my child has additional support needs (assessments)?

By law education authorities have to identify children and young people who have additional support needs and find out what those needs are. This is often done through the day to day monitoring of how children are progressing and it might be a class teacher or nursery staff who notice your child is having difficulties and might need extra support. If this happens the teacher should talk to you and your child about what support they might need. Often this will be a fairly informal process and it might happen as part of your normal contact with the school or nursery. Alternatively school or nursery staff might ask you to meet with them to discuss your child's needs. However it is done, the law says that the education authority must ask for your views and take account of them when it is deciding whether your child has additional support needs.

Case studies

Ahmed is in Primary 4 and his class teacher has noticed that he is having difficulties with reading and spelling. The teacher talks to Ahmed's parents about this at parents' night and suggests that he should be assessed to see if he has additional support needs. Ahmed's parents agree and the teacher takes this forward through the systems in place in Ahmed's school.

Gemma has just started secondary school and had an acquired brain injury aged 6 as a result of a fall. She made a good recovery but continues to have subtle cognitive difficulties affecting learning and memory and sometimes suffers from fatigue. While Gemma was at primary school these issues did not have a large impact on her learning but her parents notice that she is finding the transition to secondary school very hard and is having trouble coping with the increased work load. Gemma's parents talk to Gemma and then to the headteacher and the school agrees that she should be assessed to see whether she has additional support needs.

Although the law says that education authorities must identify your child's additional support needs it might be that you are the first to notice. If this happens a good starting point is often to talk to their class teacher (or nursery staff). Often you along with your child's teacher will be able to find ways of supporting your child by making small changes in the day to day running of the classroom or nursery. You will also be best placed to draw the school or nursery's attention to any changes in your child's circumstances, for example disruption at home.

You can also formally ask for an assessment and this may be the best course of action if your child's needs are more complex or if their school/nursery does not respond to your concerns. You have the legal right to ask for your child to be assessed to see whether they have additional support needs. The authority must carry out an assessment if you ask them to unless they decide your request is unreasonable (see box below). The law says that in most cases an education authority is expected to carry out an assessment. Therefore if you ask the authority for one it should not turn down your request without good reason.

If the authority decides not to assess your child it must explain the reasons for this and give you information about what you can do if you do not agree with the decision. This will include information about independent mediation services and the authority's Dispute Resolution system (see sections 5.7 and 5.9).

Definition of unreasonable

The Additional Support for Learning Code of Practice says that unreasonable would be 'what a third party might consider unreasonable'.

Some examples of where you could be told that asking for an assessment was unreasonable would be where the assessment:

• May not be in the best interests of the child or young person

• May not be seen as relevant given the child or young person's circumstances

• May be unnecessary as there has not been a significant change in the child's or young person's circumstances since an earlier assessment was completed

• May be within an inappropriate timescale, e.g. falling within a short time of a previous request

• May repeat assessments already carried out.

Asking for an assessment

If you decide to ask your education authority to assess your child for additional support needs you will need to start by finding out how to do that in your area. You can find out either by asking a member of staff at your child's school or by contacting the education authority contact person (see section 1.1). Your local authority must by law have information about how you can make a request for an assessment. They should also be able to give it to you in alternative formats including other languages and non-written formats such as Braille, audio or sign language.

No matter what the procedures are in your education authority you will have to request the assessment in a way that can be kept on file. This could be by writing, emailing or making a tape, CD or video recording of your request. However you choose to make your request you must say why you are asking for the assessment to be done (this could be as simple as because he/she is having problems with reading and I think he/she needs extra help with this).

If the education authority agrees to assess your child then you also have the right to ask for a specific type of assessment/s (for example a medical assessment or assessment for dyslexia) and the education authority must do this unless it is unreasonable. There are many different types of assessments (and you can ask for any of them) but the most common ones are educational, psychological, social work or medical. Although you can ask that a particular type of assessment is done you cannot specify a particular person or organisation to carry it out. For example you could ask for a social work assessment but not for it to be carried out by a specific social worker, and you could ask for a dyslexia assessment but not for this to be carried out by a particular organisation. If you do want a specific person or organisation to carry out an assessment (for example there might be a person or organisation who already knows your child well) you can talk to the education authority about this. The authority does not have to arrange this (and might not be able to) but it might be possible and it is worth asking.

You can arrange for a particular person or organisation to carry out an assessment independently of the education authority and the authority must take the results of this into account. So for example you could ask an organisation to assess your child's needs and give a report of its views to the education authority which would then have to consider the report alongside any assessments arranged by them.

If the education authority decides not to do the assessment you have asked for, it must tell you this in writing and explain the reason(s) for the decision. If you disagree with the authority's decision not to do the assessment you can use mediation services (see section 5.7) to discuss the decision and try to come to an agreement about the best way forward. You can also use the local authority's dispute resolution system to have the decision reviewed (see section 5.9). If the education authority decides not to carry out an assessment that you have asked for they must give you information about mediation and dispute resolution.

Assessments of broader needs

If your child or someone else in the household is disabled you also have the right to ask for a social work assessment to look at their wider needs (this is a right under Sections 23 and 24 of the Children Scotland Act). This type of assessment will look at all of the support your child and family might need. For example you might need specialist child care, respite services, adaptations to your home, or support for your child's non-disabled brothers or sisters.

You also have a right (under the Community Care and Health (Scotland) Act 2002) to ask for a 'Carer's Assessment' of your own needs. You have this right if your child is disabled and you are providing care on a 'substantial and regular' basis.

If you would like to request these wider assessments you can ask the professionals who are involved with you and your family or contact the social work department of your local council.

Help with asking for an assessment

If you would like help with asking for an assessment you can contact an advocacy organisation (see section 7.6 for contacts). They will be able to support you with making your request, including making contact with the education authority to find out how you can ask for an assessment.

What will assessment involve?

Assessments can be carried out in an informal way, for example through the normal daily monitoring of your child's progress, or can involve a more formal process where a specialist would be involved in working with your child to try to find out what their needs are. Whether assessment is formal or informal it should involve discussions with you, your child and the staff who are involved with your child (e.g. class teacher, support for learning staff or foster carer). The assessment process should not be negative and it should be as much about your child's strengths as it is about identifying their needs.

When you ask for an assessment the education authority should give you contact details of the person who will be looking after your case and they will be able to keep you updated. This could be a member of staff at your child's school or nursery or it could be a health or social work professional. It is part of this person's job to keep you informed so do not hesitate to contact them.

You have the right to be present at medical assessments and you will generally be able to be with your child during other types of assessment unless there is good reason for you not to be (for example an assessment could involve talking to your child about their situation at home and they might feel more able to do this privately). Your child can decide that they would prefer you were not present at a medical assessment if they have legal capacity (see section 1.7). It is a good idea to talk to your child about any assessments they will be having and it may be possible to come to a decision you are both happy with. Most children and parents will find it helpful to discuss assessments with each other and with the professionals involved to make sure they fully understand the purpose of the assessment and what will be involved.

Whenever an assessment of any kind is being done you and your child should expect that:

• Your child is seen as a whole person and that all parts of their life and needs are taken into account

• You and your child are asked for your views and these are taken into account

• You are fully informed about the purpose of any assessment, what will be involved and are asked to agree to the assessment being done

• The people involved in arranging and carrying out the assessment/s work in partnership with you will do the best for your child's health, development and welfare

• Assessments interfere as little as possible with you and your child's life and are not carried out unnecessarily

• Assessments are sensitive to any particular issues that may affect your child and do not discriminate, for example on the grounds of race, disability, gender, sexual orientation, language, religion / belief or age.

Main types of assessment

• Psychological assessment – normally carried out by an educational psychologist (possibly with advice or information from another type of psychologist such as clinical or occupational). This will identify your child's strengths and weaknesses and can look at issues such as their thinking, reading and problem solving skills

• Medical assessment – could be carried out by a wide range of professionals including a GP, nurse, speech and language therapist, occupational therapist, physiotherapist or orthopist. This type of assessment would look at health or medical issues that could affect your child's education, for example if your child was making less progress with speech and language than their peers or had mobility difficulties

• Social work assessment – carried out by a social worker. This would look at particular issues in your child's life that might be affecting his/her ability to learn. For example this might include mental or physical health problems in the family, child protection concerns, offending behaviour or your child having suffered a bereavement. If consideration was being given to placing your child in residential education a social work assessment would normally be carried out (see section 6.3)

• Assessment for a particular condition – you can also ask for your child to be assessed to see whether they have a specific condition (such as dyslexia, autistic spectrum disorder or acquired brain injury). This might involve one or more of the types of assessments described above.

Timescales

If you ask for an assessment your request should be acknowledged as soon as possible and the education authority should try to meet your request within 4 weeks. The education authority should take all steps possible to avoid delay to this timescale.

What if I disagree with the authority's decision to assess my child?

Usually the decision to carry out an assessment will be discussed and agreed by you and the education, health or social work staff involved with your child. However a situation could arise where you disagree with the education authority's decision to assess your child. If you have concerns about an assessment being done the education authority must listen to these and take them seriously. It might be possible for you and the education authority to reach an agreement by discussing your concerns and the authority's reasons for wanting to assess your child. You can use a supporter or advocate to help you with this (see section 5.6) and it might help to use independent mediation (section 5.7) to do this, especially if the relationship between you and the authority has become difficult or has broken down. If an agreement cannot be reached the authority will usually go forward with the information it already has about your child.

Medical assessments

Medical assessments differ from other types of assessment – If a medical assessment will involve any kind of medical procedure or examination then it cannot be done without consent. Your child has the right to give or refuse consent as long as they have legal capacity (see section 1.7). If your child does not have legal capacity then your consent would be needed before a medical assessment could go ahead. For information on your child receiving medical treatment at school see section 6.5.

Part 3:
Providing additional support

3.1 What happens if my child has additional support needs?

If your child has additional support needs the education authority must, by law, provide him or her with 'adequate and efficient' support so that he/she is able to benefit from education (see section 2.1 for definition of benefit from education). If your child has additional support needs and you do not think the support they are being provided with is 'adequate and efficient' then you can complain using the education authority's dispute resolution system (see section 5.9). You can also use dispute resolution if the authority assesses your child and decides they have additional support needs and you disagree with this.

The kind of support your child receives will be decided by the school or nursery along with you, your child and any other relevant people (for example a health professional or social worker). Your child's school or nursery will probably use what is called a 'staged intervention system' (most schools and nurseries do). This simply means that the nursery/school will try to deal with any difficulties your child has as early as it can and with the least possible interruption or interference with their life. The idea of this type of system is to ensure that your child is given the support they need (and that any difficulties are not left to get worse) but that it is not out of proportion to their needs. It should mean that your child does not have unnecessary assessments or a higher level of support than they need.

Example of how staged intervention might work

- Your child's teacher identifies which of his/her pupils need more attention and support than their classmates

- The teacher is given help and advice from other school staff, particularly support for learning staff, on how to support your child in the classroom

- If your child's needs are still not being met his/her teacher discusses this with you and other education staff from outwith your child's school (for example an educational psychologist)

- Support is put in place for your child and this is kept under review to make sure it is working (this might be done through an Individualised Educational Programme or IEP, see section 3.4 for more on how your child's support may be planned and monitored)

- If the support that has been put in place is not working then the school might decide to involve other services, such as social work, health or a voluntary sector organisation

- If your child then starts receiving support from a non-education service and they have multiple or complex needs that are expected to continue for more than a year they would have a co-ordinated support plan (CSP) to plan and monitor this (see section 3.5).

3.2 What support might be put in place for my child?

Support from within the school/nursery

There is a wide range of support that your child's school or nursery could provide and the level and type of additional support must be decided according to the individual needs of your child. It is not possible to say precisely what or how much additional help your child has the right to receive but the law does say that it must enable them to benefit from education (see section 2.1).

This could be a very low level of support, for example where the teacher or nursery staff are able to make small changes in order to meet your child's needs. An example of this would be where your child was falling behind with their work but simply needed some extra attention during lessons to catch up with their peers. Your child could also receive help from an auxiliary or a learning support assistant who might give them support during lessons and help with particular subjects they find difficult. Similarly if your child is ahead of his/her classmates then the school might be able to give them more advanced work that acknowledges their abilities and adds challenges to the curriculum.

Case studies

Thomas is in Primary 3 and his parents are worried that he seems to be having trouble with reading and writing. They talk to Thomas's teacher after school who tells them Thomas is only having minor difficulties but that they will keep an eye on it. A couple of months later the situation has still not improved and Thomas's parents decide to ask for him to be assessed to see whether he has additional support needs. An assessment is carried out by an educational psychologist who says that Thomas has mild learning difficulties and needs extra support. The school arranges for Thomas's parents to meet with the head teacher and learning support teacher and it is decided that Thomas will be given an hour session with the learning support teacher each week. This support will be monitored through an Individualised Educational Programme (IEP) and if Thomas's parents or the learning support teacher do not think it is working it will be discussed and changed.

Support from outwith the school/nursery

If your child has more complex needs they might need support that cannot be provided from within their school. If this is the case then the school must arrange for support to be brought in. This might be support from another part of the education authority (for example a speech and language therapist who visits different schools or nurseries).

Your child might have other needs which have an effect on their education. For example he/she could have health issues or have difficult social circumstances. If these other areas of your child's life have an impact on their ability to learn then the education authority must, by law, arrange for support to be given by the appropriate service. This might mean that the local health authority or social work department is asked (by the education authority) to help them support your child at school and the health or social work service must do this. Your child may also receive help from a specialist voluntary organisation (see section 7.6 for contacts).

If your child needs support from outwith the education authority they m ay have a co-ordinated support plan (CSP) to help this support to be planned and delivered.

For more information about CSPs see Section 3.5.

Examples of additional support that might be put in place for your child

- Extra attention from the class teacher or nursery staff
- Adapting the teaching style to complement your own approach at home, for example if you use a particular learning programme then it might be possible for the school/nursery to incorporate this into the way they teach your child
- Help from an auxiliary or learning support assistant so that your child receives one to one support during lessons and at break times
- Support staff coming to your site if you are from a Gypsy/Traveller community to help your child with specific skills such as literacy or numeracy
- Your child being given more advanced / challenging work in a subject in which they are ahead of their peers
- Support from a voluntary organisation specialising in a particular disability
- Psychiatric support if your child has mental health difficulties

- Specialist equipment
- Counselling from a specialist organisation if your child is coping with the death of a loved one
- Time with an English as an Additional Language Teacher (often called an EAL Teacher).

Unreasonable expenditure

While the law says that the education authority must put support in place for your child if they have additional support needs, it does not have to do anything which involves spending an unreasonable amount.

The law does not say what is meant by unreasonable expenditure but the Additional Support for Learning Code of Practice gives advice on what this could mean. It says that it must be judged on a case by case basis and gives a few examples of when particular types of support might not be given because the cost would be too high:

- The costs would be very high compared to how much your child would benefit from the support
- The same benefits could be achieved at a significantly lower cost
- The cost would be high (for example for building new facilities) but would not be particularly beneficial for the wider community

The Code makes clear that cost should not be the main consideration when an authority is making decisions about how to support your child. If the authority does refuse to provide your child with a particular service or facility on the grounds that it would mean spending an unreasonable amount it must tell you this and explain its decision.

Case studies

Below are a few examples of the kind of process you and your child might go through if they have additional support needs.

Jasmine is in her second year of secondary school when her mother begins to suffer from mental health problems. Jasmine starts missing a lot of school because she is caring for her mother. Her year head becomes concerned and speaks to Jasmine and her parents about the situation at home. After discussions between Jasmine, her parents and her head teacher her family agree that the school should contact the local social work department so that they can arrange for a carer to support Jasmine's mother during the day. Support is put in place for Jasmine's mother and the school arrange for Jasmine to receive support from a young carers project.

Paul is in Primary 5 and is ahead of his classmates in maths. His parents are concerned that he is getting bored and is not being offered challenging activities, but are unsure about how to approach the school. They get in touch with an advocacy organisation (see section 7.6 for contacts) who contact the school on their behalf and arrange a meeting between the head teacher and Paul's parents (which the advocate also attends). At the meeting it is agreed that Paul should be assessed for additional support needs. The assessment is done by an educational psychologist who says that Paul has additional support needs and that he must be given maths work tailored to his level. Paul's school works with the local secondary school to do this.

3.3 What professionals might be involved with me and my child?

There are many different people who could be involved in supporting your child with their learning. These include staff based at your child's school or nursery as well as peripatetic staff (for example educational psychologists or English as an Additional Language teachers, who work across a number of schools or nurseries) and professionals from the health service (such as speech and language therapists), social work department or voluntary organisations. You and your child should be fully informed about all the professionals you come into contact with and what their roles are. If you are unclear about the role of anyone who is involved in supporting your child you should feel free to ask them or someone else (for example the person in your local authority who is responsible for providing you with advice and information, see section 5.2). Some of the people that you and your child might come into contact with are described in section 7.4.

3.4 How will the school plan and monitor my child's support?

Once support has been put in place the school must monitor it to make sure it is working for your child. The way that your child's support is planned and monitored will vary to some extent from school to school and according to what level and type of additional support your child needs. All education authorities must have information about the way they monitor and review additional support needs. You can get a copy of this by contacting the education department of your local council (it might also be available on the council website). Regardless of how your child's support is planned you should be kept fully informed about learning goals and objectives and what support will be put in place to help your child achieve these. You and your child should be given the opportunity to work in partnership with the school or nursery to decide what these goals and objectives should be and how they can be reached.

The three main types of plans that are used are: personal learning plans (PLPs), Individualised Educational Programmes (IEPs) and co-ordinated support plans (CSPs). The boxes on the next page show how these plans relate to each other and then each one is described in further detail.

Personal learning plan (PLP)	Individualised Educational Programme (IEP)	Co-ordinated support plan (CSP)
All children and young people with additional support needs should be involved in personal learning planning. A personal learning plan will set out manageable and realistic goals and be used to involve your child in planning their own learning.	Children and young people with more complex needs will have an individualised educational programme as well as their PLP. The IEP will set out more specific, short and long term, learning objectives for your child. It will also give details of what additional support your child needs.	Some children and young people with complex or multiple needs will have a co-ordinated support plan in addition to their PLP and IEP. The CSP is the only one of the three plans that is a legal document. It sets out specific long term objectives and the support needed to achieve these. You can appeal to an additional support needs tribunal about issues relating to your child's CSP (see section 5.10)

Personal learning plan (PLP)

If your child requires only a low level of additional support this is likely to be monitored by their nursery or class teacher in the course of day to day teaching. All children and young people have their education planned and monitored in some way and for most this will be done through personal learning planning (all children who need additional support with learning should be involved in personal learning planning). A PLP is not a legal document, it is a practical tool which sets out your child's goals in terms of learning and personal development. It is meant to help you and the school or nursery to work together and above all to support your child to be involved in their own learning.

Individualised Educational Programme (IEP)

If your child needs lessons to be adapted significantly their support is likely to be planned and monitored using an IEP. An IEP will set out short term goals (for example what your child is aiming to achieve over the course of a few weeks or months) and give details of what support will be put in place to help your child reach these. The IEP should give detailed information about targets, support and your child's day to day learning and teaching and might involve input from non-education professionals. As a parent you should be given the chance to be involved in your child's IEP including taking part in decisions about what they will be taught, the approach to learning and teaching that will work best for them, and looking at how your child's school learning can be reinforced and supported at home. Your education authority may have information about the circumstances in which they would use an IEP and you can ask the education authority contact person for this (see section 1.1).

An IEP is not a legal document which means that writing a particular type of support into an IEP does not put an obligation on the education authority to provide it. However the authority must by law provide your child with the additional support they need (see section 2.1) regardless of what type of education plan/s they have.

Co-ordinated support plan (CSP)

A CSP is a legal document which contains information about your child's long term learning aims and the support that is needed to help them reach these. There are specific legal criteria for which children will have a CSP and if your child meets these criteria the education authority is legally required to prepare one.

You can ask your education authority to assess your child for a CSP and the authority must do this unless your request is unreasonable (see section 3.2 for definition of unreasonable and section 2.4 for details of how to request assessments). In most cases you should find out within 4 weeks whether or not the authority will prepare a CSP for your child (see Timescales on P43 for further information). If you disagree with the education authority's decision of whether or not to prepare a CSP you can appeal to an Additional Support Needs Tribunal (see section 5.10).

CSPs are more complicated than PLPs or IEPs so we will focus on them in detail in the following few sections of this handbook.

3.5 How is a co-ordinated support plan (CSP) prepared (i.e. opened), co-ordinated and monitored?

There are legal guidelines about the process of preparing and reviewing a CSP and if you disagree with the education authority in relation to a CSP you can appeal to an Additional Support Needs Tribunal (see section 5.10). This section guides you through the CSP system.

Criteria for preparing a CSP

The education authority is legally required to prepare a CSP for your child if:

- the education authority is responsible for their education (in other words they are of school age and attend a school run by the authority, or are receiving their legal entitlement to part-time nursery education)

  AND

- their additional support needs are caused by a complex factor/s or by multiple factors (a number of issues which combine to have a significant adverse effect on their learning)

  AND

- their additional support needs are likely to continue for longer than a year

  AND

- their needs mean they require significant additional support

  AND

- they need support to be provided from outwith the education department (for example from social work or the health service).

In other words your child will have a CSP if the situation leading to their additional support needs is complex (for example a complex disability or health issue) or if there are a number of different factors making it difficult for them to get the most out of education (for example where a child is a young carer who also suffers from mental health problems and has dyslexia) (see section 2.2 for more on 'complex' and 'multiple' factors). In addition to this their needs must be expected to last for more than a year and mean that they need 'significant support'. Your child must also need support that cannot be provided by education services alone.

The law does not define the term 'significant support' and there is not a precise level above which your child would be said to need significant support. However there is guidance on the definition which suggests that your child would need significant support if they needed provision that was at the higher end of what is available. This would be judged in terms of the frequency, type and intensity of the support and how crucial it is to your child reaching their education objectives. The Additional Support for Learning Code of Practice suggests that a child who is placed full-time in a special school would be said to need significant support, as would a pupil in full-time mainstream school who uses communication aids and receives input from specialist staff.

Case studies

The case studies below offer a few examples of situations in which your child might or might not have a CSP opened.

Craig is in second year of secondary school and lives with his father who has drug and alcohol problems. Craig is also being bullied at school and this has resulted in him experiencing mental health difficulties. The school decides to assess him for additional support needs and to decide if a CSP should be opened. It is decided that a CSP should be opened to plan Craig's support as he has multiple factors which affect his ability to benefit from school, these are likely to continue for more than a year and will need significant ongoing support including from the local social work department.

Stacey is in primary 2 and has cerebral palsy and as a result has mobility difficulties and learning difficulties. An assessment is done and it is decided that a CSP will be opened as her disability is complex, will last more than a year and she needs a high level of input from health professionals in order to benefit from education.

Ben is in primary 6 and has a visual impairment and dyslexia which means that his classes have to be adapted and he receives help from a learning support assistant. He is assessed and (although his needs will last longer than a year, are caused by multiple factors and mean he needs significant support) it is decided that he does not meet the criteria for a CSP as he does not need support from outwith education services.

Assessing for a CSP

Clearly the criteria for a CSP are open to interpretation and the education authority will decide whether or not to prepare one for your child based on information from assessments (see section 2.4). There may well be enough information available from assessments your child has already had (for example to see whether they have additional support needs) in which case no further formal assessments will be carried out. In this situation the assessment for a CSP will involve the education authority looking at all the information and deciding whether or not your child fits the CSP criteria. However further assessments may be required and you have the right to request these as long as they relate directly to finding out whether your child needs a CSP.

You and your child should be involved in the assessment for a CSP and in particular in deciding how much something affects his/her ability to benefit from school or nursery. Legal guidance (Additional Support for Learning Code of Practice) stresses that the effect a factor has will vary from child to child and that those best placed to decide what impact a situation or issue will have on your child are you, your child, and professionals who know your child well.

If your education authority decides to assess your child for a CSP the authority must tell you they plan to do this. The authority must give you information about:

• which agencies and departments will be contacted for views, advice and information

• any assessments or examinations that will be involved

• your right to ask for particular types of assessment/s

• your right to provide advice and information to be considered in the education authority's decision of whether to prepare a CSP

• your right to advice and information about your child's CSP assessment

• your involvement in the process

• the expected timescale.

Preparing a CSP

If your child needs a CSP you, and they, have a right to be involved in preparing this, to have your opinions noted in the CSP and to receive a copy of the final CSP. Once the decision has been made that a CSP should be prepared for your child someone from the education authority will be designated to arrange this (this could be your child's teacher or someone else from their school or may be someone from another part of the education department). This person will consult with you, your child and all relevant professionals about your child's needs, educational objectives and support. This might happen by holding a CSP meeting with everyone present to discuss the content of the CSP. After initial discussions the designated person will write a draft CSP and ask for comments from you, your child and other professionals (again this might be done by arranging a CSP meeting). A final version of the CSP will be agreed and you will be given a copy. A date for reviewing the CSP will be set (this will normally be 12 months) and a CSP co-ordinator will be appointed (this may happen earlier in the process). All those involved in supporting your child will monitor the CSP until the formal review.

The Additional Support for Learning Code of Practice sets out the process of preparing a CSP in the chart (over the page):

Criteria　　　　　　　　Evidence

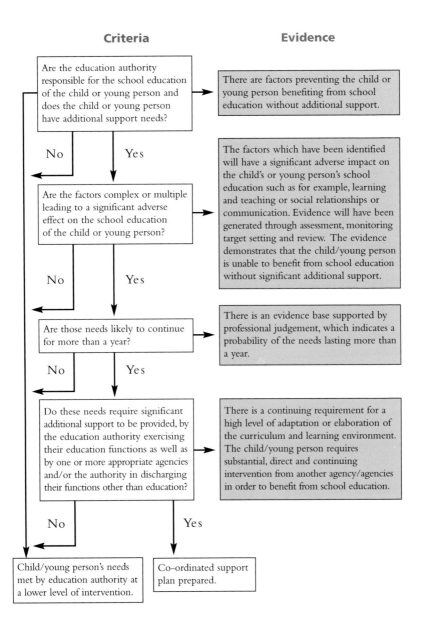

Are the education authority responsible for the school education of the child or young person and does the child or young person have additional support needs?

There are factors preventing the child or young person benefiting from school education without additional support.

No　　　Yes

Are the factors complex or multiple leading to a significant adverse effect on the school education of the child or young person?

The factors which have been identified will have a significant adverse impact on the child's or young person's school education such as for example, learning and teaching or social relationships or communication. Evidence will have been generated through assessment, monitoring target setting and review. The evidence demonstrates that the child/young person is unable to benefit from school education without significant additional support.

No　　　Yes

Are those needs likely to continue for more than a year?

There is an evidence base supported by professional judgement, which indicates a probability of the needs lasting more than a year.

No　　　Yes

Do these needs require significant additional support to be provided, by the education authority exercising their education functions as well as by one or more appropriate agencies and/or the authority in discharging their functions other than education?

There is a continuing requirement for a high level of adaptation or elaboration of the curriculum and learning environment. The child/young person requires substantial, direct and continuing intervention from another agency/agencies in order to benefit from school education.

No　　　Yes

Child/young person's needs met by education authority at a lower level of intervention.

Co-ordinated support plan prepared.

CSP contents

The Additional Support for Learning Code of Practice sets out what information your child's CSP must contain (see section 5.10 for details of what parts of the CSP can be appealed to an additional support needs tribunal):

- Details of the factor/s that cause your child to need additional support
- The longer term educational objectives that your child is aiming to achieve (shorter term objectives will be detailed in your child's IEP, see section 3.4). The objectives can be broader than just academic aspects of your child's education but they must require additional support to be put in place and co-ordinated. For example your child might have an objective of learning to eat independently and need to be supported by school catering staff and a speech and language therapist to do this
- The additional support required to achieve these objectives and details of who (i.e. which agency or service) will provide the support
- Name of the school your child is to attend
- Details of CSP co-ordinator (including name, address and telephone number)
- Details of the person within the local authority who you can contact for further advice and information.

Your child's CSP must, by law, include the above information. However, the Additional Support for Learning Code of Practice lists the other information it is likely to contain:

- Biographical and contact details for your child
- Contact details for you and anyone else who shares responsibility for the care of your child
- A profile of your child – the purpose of this is to build a holistic pen picture of your child. It should focus on the positive aspects of his/her life, for example, his/her skills and capabilities. It may also include information about the school he/she attends, the

curriculum followed, other planning in place, his/her favourite activities, and how he/she likes to learn

• Your comments on any aspects of the CSP process as well as the CSP itself

• Your child's comments on any aspects of the CSP process as well as the CSP itself

• A review timetable.

When a CSP is being prepared the process should begin by looking at what your child's educational objectives should be and then deciding what support he/she needs to reach these. This should be based on assessment information and discussion with you, your child and relevant professionals. Availability of support should not be the starting point for your child's CSP and should not influence what the educational objectives are. Once the objectives are agreed the education authority has a legal requirement to provide the additional support needed to achieve these. The CSP should give clear, detailed information on what this additional support will be and which agency or service will be providing it. The Additional Support for Learning Code of Practice gives the example that:

Statements such as 'learning support as necessary' or 'speech and language therapy as required' are too vague to be helpful. A statement such as the following provides a clearer idea about what is being provided:

• Voluntary agency to provide group work in school for 2 hours per week, approximately, for 1 term

• Speech and language therapist and classroom assistant will provide weekly therapy within a small group setting for 6 weeks followed by a specific programme being supported within the mainstream curriculum by the teacher and classroom assistant with a review of outcomes at the end of term.

The objectives will be long term (generally what your child is expected to achieve in around a year) but should also include 'milestones' for monitoring progress throughout the year. Shorter term objectives will be in your child's IEP.

CSP co-ordinator

Your education authority must appoint someone as your child's CSP co-ordinator. This person is likely to come from within the education authority although the authority can appoint another professional if this is more appropriate for your child (for example if your child is in pre-school and needs additional support because of a medical issue it might make more sense for a health professional such as their paediatrician to co-ordinate their CSP). The CSP co-ordinator is responsible for monitoring the support being provided to your child and for making sure that the support identified in the CSP is delivered. If there is a problem it is the co-ordinator's job to respond to this and they must sort out any disruption to your child's support. For example if services being delivered from an agency outwith education break down the CSP co-ordinator must work with that agency to put those services back in place as quickly as possible.

CSP co-ordinator

The Additional Support for Learning Code of Practice lists what else a CSP co-ordinator should do:

- Maintain regular contact with you and your child
- Be familiar with the school your child attends
- Have a working knowledge of relevant service policies and practices
- Have experience of working with children and young people with additional support needs
- Have experience of compiling and implementing educational support plans (such as IEPs) or health and care plans
- Be able to work with other agencies.

The education authority should try not to change your child's CSP co-ordinator if it can be avoided. However if the co-ordinator does change (for example this might happen if your co-ordinator changes jobs or when your child moves from primary to secondary school) you should be told about this and you must be sent an updated copy of the CSP with the new co-ordinator's details.

CSP Review

Your child's CSP must be reviewed at least every 12 months. The authority may carry out a review earlier if your child's needs or circumstances have changed since the CSP was prepared. You can also ask for a review to be done before the 12 month review date and the authority must do this unless they consider your request to be unreasonable (see section 3.2).

The authority must tell you if they intend to review your child's CSP earlier than the original review date and ask for your views. The review will look at how far your child's educational objectives have been reached, your child's current needs, and setting new educational objectives and deciding what support will be required to achieve them.

Once the review has been done the authority must tell you the outcome, give you a copy of the updated CSP and give you information about your right to appeal to an Additional Support Needs Tribunal if you disagree with the content (see section 5.10).

Timescales

The education authority has a total of 16 weeks to complete your child's CSP. The 16 week period begins on the date that the authority send you notification that they intend to assess your child for a CSP and ends on the date the authority sends you a copy of the completed CSP. Within this time the authority should establish whether or not your child meets the criteria for a CSP, notify you of the decision to prepare a CSP, and prepare the CSP.

Where possible the education authority should tell you within the first 4 weeks of the 16 week time period whether or not they intend to prepare a CSP for your child.

There are circumstances where the 16 week time limit could be extended (for example if a particular assessment cannot be completed in time) but the education authority is expected to do as much as possible to ensure that this does not happen. If it seems that completing your child's CSP is going to take longer than 16 weeks the authority must tell you this, explain the reason for the delay and set a new date for the CSP to be completed. Even if the preparation of your child's CSP is delayed it should not take more than 24 weeks in total.

If the preparation of your child's CSP is delayed beyond the 16 week time limit you can complain to an Additional Support Needs Tribunal (see section 5.10) and the tribunal will decide whether the delay is reasonable.

Timescales for review of the CSP

The education authority must complete a CSP review within 12 weeks of the review date unless there is an unavoidable delay (for example if an assessment is needed and this cannot be done within the 12 week time limit). If there is a delay the education authority must tell you the reasons for this and agree a new date. If the review of your child's CSP takes longer than 12 weeks you can complain to an Additional Support Needs Tribunal (see section 5.10) which will judge whether the delay is reasonable.

Moving area

If you are moving home you may move into a new education authority and the new authority will take over responsibility for your child's support. If you are not sure whether you are moving into a new authority area you can contact your local council which will be able to tell you (you will find contact details in the phone book or by calling directory inquiries).

If your child has a CSP and you move to a different education authority the CSP will move with your child. The education authority you are moving from must pass on the CSP within 4 weeks. The 4 weeks start from the date that the education authority was told that your child would be moving, unless they were not notified in which case the 4 weeks start from the date the authority found out that your child has moved. The new authority must treat the CSP as if they had prepared it although they can carry out an immediate review. The new authority must tell you that they have received the CSP and (at the same time if possible) inform you of who your child's new co-ordinator will be and who within the authority you can contact for advice and information (see section 5.2).

3.6 How do education plans relate to other children's plans?

Your child may have more than one plan setting out their needs and the support they receive. They might have one or more plans for areas of their life other than education and any education plan should link into these where possible. For example if your child has a health or social work plan which contains education objectives then these should be the same as the objectives in an Individualised Educational Programme (IEP) or a Co-ordinated Support Plan (CSP) (unless there is good reason for them to be different). This is particularly important if your child is 'looked-after' by the local authority as they will then have a statutory care plan which will include information about their education needs. Similarly there are many different types of health plans and these should overlap with your child's IEP and/or CSP where they refer to education needs or objectives.

The Scottish Executive is in the process of trying to improve the way that different children's plans fit together. The system that is being developed is called the 'Integrated Assessment Framework (IAF)'. Work on this was still underway at the time of writing this handbook but the general aim is to make sure that different services work together so that all children and young people get the support they need, when they need it, without having to have lots of overlapping plans or assessments.

Part 4:
Stages of schooling

The education system, and your child's needs, change at different stages. This section covers what happens in the early years (pre-school) through to starting or moving schools and then to leaving school. There is also a section on home education, where parents educate their own children at home.

Many of the difficulties parents face in trying to secure the right support for their child happen during transitions – for example when moving from primary to secondary and then leaving school. In law, these are called 'changes in education'. Problems can also arise when children move schools, for example if you move to a different education authority area.

Education authorities should make sure that changes to a child's education are as smooth as possible. To help them do that, they should request information and advice from other agencies (for example, the school your child is moving to) 12 months before your child is expected to have a change in education. These other agencies should provide this information 6 months before your child is expected to move schools. For changes in pre-school education the timescale is that the authority should request information from the pre-school 6 months before your child would start school and that all information should be passed on 3 months before your child starts school. Before the education authority passes on any information on your child, they have to ask for your permission.

The Additional Support for Learning Code of Practice outlines good practice in preparing for changes to education:

• Transition planning should be embedded within the education authority's policies and procedures for additional support needs

- Other agencies, such as health and social work services, Careers Scotland, Further Education Colleges and Institutions of Higher Education should also be involved in transition planning where required
- The child's or young person's views should be sought and taken into account when discussing changes in school education
- Parents should be part of the planning process, and their views should be sought, and taken account of, and they should receive support, as required during the transition process
- Early consultation should take place with the school or post-school provision, which the child or young person will be attending
- Schools should plan to ensure that the necessary support is in place for children who have additional support needs to help them through the transition phase to their new school
- Professionals from all agencies working with the child and family should plan in good time for transition to future services
- Transition should be co-ordinated by a relevant person known to the child or young person and their family
- Where a child or young person has a co-ordinated support plan, any anticipated change in the statutory co-ordinator should be discussed with the child or young person, and parents, as far in advance of the change as possible.

4.1 Transitions

This section discusses the main stages of schooling and transitions that your child is likely to go through during their education.

Under 3 years old

When your child is under 3, you are most likely to be in contact with health professionals, as the NHS provides a universal service to all families with young children. Your health visitor or GP will check your child for any problems with their hearing or sight and other disorders such as speech and language or delays in walking. Similarly they may discover that your child is reaching developmental milestones earlier than expected. If your child is under 3 and you have any concerns about whether they might have additional support needs, you should contact your health visitor or GP to discuss this.

The obligation to provide additional support only applies to pre-school and school education, not to other early years services. Education authorities can provide support for children who are under 3 years old and have additional needs but they do not have to do so. However, education authorities do have to provide additional support for disabled children under the age of 3 (as defined by the Disability Discrimination Act, see section 6.1) who have additional support needs.

If your child has a disability the NHS should inform the education authority. The education authority can assess whether or not your child has additional support needs (the Additional Support for Learning Code of Practice says that the authority should do this unless there is a good reason not to). If an assessment is done and the authority finds that your child has additional support needs, it must provide support.

Identifying additional support in the early years

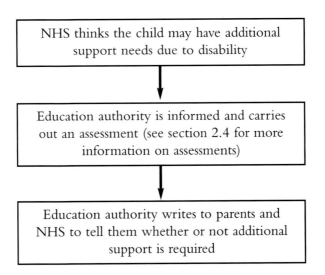

NHS thinks the child may have additional support needs due to disability

Education authority is informed and carries out an assessment (see section 2.4 for more information on assessments)

Education authority writes to parents and NHS to tell them whether or not additional support is required

The Additional Support for Learning Code of Practice says that the staff from the NHS and the education authority should work together and try to make sure that you do not have to repeat the same information to different professionals, they will try to share what information they can with each other to make sure that they provide the best support for your child (see section 5.2 for more information on data protection issues).

If the education authority decides that your child has additional support needs arising from their disability, they should then agree with you what support will be provided, including an 'action plan' with details on how you can get involved. They should also provide you with a 'key worker' who will be the main person that you deal with if you need to talk to someone about the support that is being provided for your child.

If the education authority decides that your child does not have additional support needs arising from their disability, and you disagree, you may want to go to dispute resolution to challenge their decision (see section 5.9 for further information on dispute resolution).

Pre-school (3 and 4 year olds)

When your child is receiving their entitlement to free pre-school education provided by the education authority (see box) the system for additional support needs is the same as for school education. In this situation education authorities must provide support to all children with additional support needs, not just disabled children (see section 2.1 for more information).

Free pre-school education

If your child is aged 3 or 4 they have the right to a free place at a nursery for 12.5 hours a week, usually taken as five 2.5 hour sessions. The nursery might be based in a primary school or it could be a private nursery or one run by a voluntary organisation. You do not have to send your child to pre-school education. It is voluntary, but most parents now make use of the free entitlement.

Many disabled children will be identified in the early years by health professionals, however other disorders such as speech and language difficulties, emotional and behavioural difficulties and other communication or development problems may not be picked up until your child is in pre-school education.

In pre-school education the assessment and services provided are likely to be similar to those for primary or secondary pupils. See section 2.4 for further information.

If your child does not attend pre-school provided by the education authority (for example they are looked after at home or they are in a private nursery), and you think they may have additional support needs, the education authority can assess them and provide support but they do not have to do so. This is because it may be difficult for them to provide additional support when they are not in contact with your child. Information on how to ask for an assessment can be found in section 2.4.

Starting school

Children normally start school at 4 or 5 years old in Scotland. If there is a good reason why your child should start school earlier or later, you can ask the education authority to allow this. The education authority may let your child start school earlier or later and if you request this the authority may ask you to make a placing request (see section 4.4). This allows them to see your reasons for wanting your child to start school earlier or later.

If your child has additional support needs that were identified in the early years or at pre-school, you should be involved in discussions about whether or not their needs can be met at the local primary school and what additional support is required. Education authorities have a duty to educate children in mainstream schools, in all but exceptional circumstances. The majority of children with additional support needs will be educated at the local primary school. See section 6.4 for more information on mainstream education.

Primary to secondary school

The type of transition support will depend on your child's additional support needs, for example the secondary school may make sure that your child is placed in a class with friends or they might arrange for an advance trip to the school to make sure that it is fully accessible to your child. For more complex or multiple needs, the planning may involve making sure that the right type of support staff are available in the new school, for example classroom assistants or speech and language therapists.

If you think that your child is not ready for secondary school, you can ask the education authority to allow them to stay on at primary school for one extra year. In some cases, teachers might suggest this to you, but if you think it would help your child the school should be able to arrange this.

If your child is moving to a different education authority school for secondary education then the education authority can request information and advice from that education authority, and from the NHS.

Leaving school

If your child is preparing to leave school, they may need additional support to go on to employment, training, further or higher education. The principles of good practice in the Additional Support for Learning Code of Practice state that you should be involved in planning for your child leaving school and that you should receive support to do this if you need it.

The education authority has to help prepare post-school services for your child. This planning should take place throughout their final year at school. This applies to all children with additional support needs, not just those with a co-ordinated support plan.

To help them plan for services after your child leaves school, the education authority can ask for advice and information from:

• Any other local authority
• Any NHS Board

- Careers Scotland
- Further Education Colleges
- Higher Education Institutions.

By law these agencies must help the education authority plan for the change in your child's education. The education authority must ask for this advice and information 12 months before your child leaves school and should get your permission before doing this.

Six months before your child leaves school the education authority must provide information to the agencies that will be taking over responsibility for your child's support. This is likely to be information about your child's needs and what support they received at school. The authority can only give out this information with your consent, or if your child is 16 or over, with their consent.

Schools are under a legal obligation to provide careers education so when your child is preparing to leave school, the school will have a programme of careers education in place for them. Careers education may include discussions with a careers adviser, talks on different types of careers, work experience and visits to colleges or universities. The school may also provide classes on life skills, for example, on money management or living on your own. Some of this will be during personal and social education classes but if necessary, the school might provide additional support to your child to help them prepare for leaving school.

In addition to the help provided by the education authority, Careers Scotland can help. Careers Scotland aims to help all young people who want to get into education, training or employment. Careers Scotland has staff with special skills that can help anyone with additional support needs to:

- look at their own interests, skills and strengths
- understand the range of options open to them
- develop realistic and achievable career plans
- develop job seeking skills if appropriate
- make applications for college and university courses

- apply for current job or training vacancies
- link with other helpful organisations and agencies.

Contact details for Careers Scotland can be found at the end of this handbook (see section 7.6).

Case study

Joshua is 16 and goes to his local secondary school. He has social, emotional and behavioural difficulties but the school was able to provide support for him and he got good results in his Standard Grades. He doesn't have a co-ordinated support plan but the school started working with him to plan what he wanted to do after he left school. After discussing his options with a careers adviser, Joshua decided he wanted to go to college and study joinery at the end of his 5th year at school, just under a year away. With Joshua's permission, his guidance teacher contacted the local college and the school and the college began to discuss what sort of help Joshua might need to help him get the most out of college. They also arranged a day trip to the college for Joshua to see what it was like and to meet the staff. Around six months before Joshua was due to start college the staff had all the information they needed about his needs to help them plan his support and he had a smooth transition to the college in the autumn.

4.2 Placing requests

Normally the education authority will suggest that your child attends a particular local primary school. They will write and tell you which one. Your child does not have to go to that school, though, and you have the right to put in a 'placing request' if you think that a different school would better meet the needs of your child. For example, a different school may be better equipped to support your child, or may have a specialism in a subject that your child shows particular aptitude for. The system for placing requests for a child with additional support needs is slightly different from that for other children.

You can make placing requests if you would like your child to be educated by:

- any school run by a Scottish education authority
- a special school
- a school in England, Wales and Northern Ireland that is wholly or mainly for children who have additional support needs
- any person that provides education for children under school age (for example, a private nursery that provides education for children with additional support needs).

You cannot make a placing request to:

- an independent school (sometimes called private schools) that is not a special school
- a school that your child has already been excluded from (i.e. they have been expelled)
- a single sex school if your child is not the sex admitted.

If you are applying to a school run by a Scottish education authority you make the placing request to the education authority that runs that school. This may be a different education authority from the authority responsible for education in the area that you live in. You do not have to check directly with the school first.

If you decide to make a placing request you have to write to the education authority with your name and address, your child's name and the name of the school you would prefer. Scottish Executive guidance on choosing a school also suggests that you give your child's age and (if already at school) the name of his or her present school and stage of education (for example, primary 1, primary 2 and so on). You do not have to give reasons for your choice of school but doing so will help the education authority make its decision. Many education authorities have specific forms for placing requests and you should contact the education authority to ask for one before making your request.

Special Schools

If your child has multiple or complex needs, the issue of whether or not to place them in a special school may come up. This might be suggested by the education authority or you may feel that a special school would be better able to meet the needs of your child. Special schools are run by the education authority and there are no fees for your child to attend a special school instead of their local primary or secondary.

Around 2 per cent of children in Scotland attend special schools. The decision to educate your child in a special school may be taken before they start school, or you may make a placing request at any time. In 2003/04, special schools accounted for 0.4 per cent of all placing requests (115 requests in total), of which 83 per cent were granted. Whenever the decision is being taken, you should be fully involved and you and your child's views should be taken into account by the education authority.

More information on special schools can be found in section 6.4.

Grant aided/independent schools

The rules for placing requests for children who have additional support needs are mostly the same as for all children. However, in addition to being able to ask that your child attend any education authority school or nursery, you can also request that your child goes to:

• an independent special school in Scotland

• an independent special school in England, Wales or Northern Ireland

• an independent special school for children under school age or

• a grant-aided special school.

Independent special schools are privately run and will have fees while grant-aided schools are given funding directly from the Scottish Executive. The grant-aided special schools in Scotland are:

• Corseford School in Renfrewshire

• Craighalbert Centre for Children with Motor Impairments in Cumbernauld

- Donaldson's College for the Deaf in Edinburgh
- East Park School in Glasgow
- Harmeny School for 8-12 year old children with severe emotional and behavioural difficulties in Edinburgh
- Royal Blind School in Edinburgh
- Stanmore House School in Lanarkshire.

To make a placing request to an independent or grant-aided special school or nursery you must make the request to the education authority for the area that you live in, as they will be paying the fees. Before making the placing request you may find it helpful to talk to the head teacher of the school that you want your child to attend. If you are thinking of sending your child to an independent or grant-aided school, in Scotland or elsewhere, you must check that they are willing to take your child before you make the request.

If the education authority accepts your placing request to an independent or grant-aided special school, then they must meet the fees and any other costs associated with placing the child in that school.

Schools outside the UK

The Additional Support for Learning Act also allows education authorities to make arrangements for a child with additional support needs to be educated at a school or other facility outwith the UK. They do not have to do this but they can if they wish. If they agree then the education authority can meet part or all of the fees, including travelling and maintenance for the child and their parent. The only restriction is that the school must be wholly or mainly for children with additional support needs. If you think that this might benefit your child you should speak to the education authority. It is unlikely that this will be used often due to pressure on education authority budgets.

Because they do not have to arrange for your child to be educated outside the UK, if the education authority does not agree to your request you cannot appeal to the education authority Appeals Committee or an Additional Support Needs Tribunal.

Reasons an education authority can refuse a placing request

The school's capacity

* It would be necessary for the education authority to employ an additional teacher

* It would cost a significant amount to alter the accommodation or facilities at the school

* If, at a future stage in your child's education, the overall numbers would mean that an extra class or extra teacher would be required

* If placing your child in the school would mean that the education authority would not have enough places to educate children who are expected to move into the school's catchment area during the school year

* If, for any other reason, the school does not have the capacity in terms of numbers.

Your child's needs

* It would be detrimental to the continuity of your child's education

* If the education provided by the school is not suited to the age, aptitude or ability of your child

* If the education authority can provide, and have offered to provide, the support in a different school, which is more appropriate once suitability and cost have been taken into account

* If the request is for a special school but placing your child there would go against the principle that children should, as far as is possible, be educated in mainstream schools.

Impact on education of other children

* It is likely that placing your child in the school would be seriously detrimental to order and discipline in the school

* It is likely to be seriously detrimental to the educational well-being of pupils attending the school.

Appeals

The education authority is required by law to allow your child to attend a different school where it is possible. The education authority can refuse a placing request on grounds relating to the capacity of the school, your child's needs, and the impact on other school pupils (see box). If one of those conditions applies, the education authority may still admit your child to the school but they do not have to. The education authority must write to you and tell you whether or not they have accepted your request.

If you have made a placing request to an education authority but have not had a response by:

- 30th April - if you made the request by 15th March and the request is to start at the school at the beginning of the school year in August; or

- 2 months after the education authority received your placing request

then it is called a 'deemed refusal'. This means that you should consider your request to be declined. The reason the system is designed in this way is to allow you appeal the education authority's decision as soon as possible and not be held up by delays in the authority processing your request.

If your placing request has been denied by the education authority you can appeal. The body you appeal to depends on the type of additional support needs your child has. If your child has:

- additional support needs but does not require a co-ordinated support plan you can appeal to the education authority Appeal Committee. The Appeal Committee is an independent body which will have three, five or seven members, including parents (usually school board members), local councillors and others with a knowledge of education in your local area. None of the members should be involved in the school that your child attends or that you have made a placing request to. The Education Authority should give you information on how to appeal to the Appeal Committee. More information on the procedures can be found in the box.

* additional support needs and does require a co-ordinated support plan (i.e. your child has a co-ordinated support plan, it has been decided that they need one or you are appealing the decision that they do not need one) you can appeal to an Additional Support Needs Tribunal (see section 5.10 for more information).

If you place your appeal with the education authority Appeal Committee but it turns out that it should be dealt with by the Additional Support Needs Tribunal, the Committee will automatically pass it to the tribunal. Staff in the education authority and the Additional Support Needs Tribunals should be able to offer you advice on where best to appeal to (see section 7.6 for contacts).

What happens if I appeal to the Education Authority Appeal Committee?

After you have written to the Appeal Committee asking for an appeal, the Appeal Committee must give you a date for the hearing within 14 days of receiving your appeal. They must also give you at least 14 days' advance notice of the hearing but it must usually be within 28 days of receiving your appeal letter.

You have the following rights at an appeal:

• the right to appear and be represented

• the right to be accompanied by up to three people (including a representative or advocate, if any)

• the right to submit a written case, as well as, or instead of, speaking to the committee.

The Chair of the Appeal Committee has control over the events and the process followed. Committee members can put questions to anyone giving evidence. Each Appeal Committee will have a Code of Practice outlining the procedures and how they are to make decisions.

The Appeal Committee must tell you its decision, in writing, within 14 days of the hearing. You should be given enough information so that you understand why the decision was taken. If they do not do this, you can ask for a statement of reasons for the decision.

If you still disagree with their decision you can appeal to the Sheriff. You have to lodge your appeal within 28 days of receiving the decision by the Appeal Committee. You should consult a solicitor who has experience of education law if you are thinking of doing this.

Taken from The A – Z Scots Education Law (SCC, 2004)

4.3 Home education and Flexi-schooling

The law says you must make sure that your child is educated but you do not have to send them to school. Some parents choose to educate their children at home. If you home educate, you have to make sure that your child receives 'suitable' and 'efficient' education – which means that it must include:

• consistent parental involvement

• recognition of your child's needs, attitudes and aspirations

• involvement in a broad spectrum of activities and

• access to appropriate resources and materials.

You do not need permission to educate your child at home if they have never attended a local authority school. However, if you are removing your child from school then you will need to get the education authority's permission. The authority is not allowed to withhold permission without reasonable cause. If you are considering home education you may want to contact Schoolhouse Home Education Association for more information (see section 7.6 for contacts). The Scottish Executive has also produced guidance on this which you may find useful (Scottish Executive, 2004, Guidance on the circumstances in which parents may choose to educate their children at home).

If you are home educating your child, you can ask the education authority to assess whether or not they have additional support needs or would require a co-ordinated support plan, but the education authority does not have to do so. If it decides not to assess your child it must inform you of its decision and tell you the reasons why. If you are still not happy with their explanation, you can go to mediation or access dispute resolution services to resolve the problem. (Further information on this can be found in sections 5.7 and 5.9).

If the education authority do carry out an assessment then they should always tell you about any additional support your child needs. The education authority may provide this support themselves but they do not have to do so.

For some children with additional support needs, Flexi-schooling might be suggested. Flexi-schooling means that you and the education authority share the job of educating your child. This may happen if parents want to start (or continue) home educating their child for only part of the week so that they can make use of the services of the education authority. Usually there will be a written contract between you and the education authority setting out what each of you will provide for the child. Flexi-schooling is only possible with the permission and support of the education authority.

> **Case study**
>
> Saskia is 7 years old and has Attention Deficit Hyperactivity Disorder. She started school at the local primary when she was 5 but she has been finding it more difficult lately because there is more formal teaching now and she has difficulty concentrating. She often disturbs the other children in the class and the teacher has reported finding it difficult to teach the other children. The school feels that a special school might be better for Saskia but her parents don't think that it would be the best option, they want her to stay with the friends she has already made and feel that the disruption of a new school might set her back. The education authority officer comes to the school to speak to Saskia's parents and the head teacher, and suggests that they think about flexi-schooling. Her parents agree to try educating Saskia at home for 3 days a week and the head teacher feels that with some rearrangement of the lesson plans and a classroom assistant they will be able to have Saskia at school for the other 2 days. The school keeps in contact with Saskia's parents so that her activities at school and home complement each other. A date is set to review the arrangement with a view to increasing the amount of time Saskia spends at school.

Part 5:

Being involved and dealing with problems

5.1 Working in partnership with your child's school

As a parent there are many ways in which you can be involved with your child's school or nursery and research shows that your involvement will help your child to do well at school. You might want to have a high level of involvement in the life of the school, for example helping out with school trips or setting up services such as an after school club, but simply having good ongoing communication between you and the school or nursery will benefit your child. If you can talk to school/nursery staff about how your child is getting on then you and they will be able to support them better and identify problems early on.

Your child's school or nursery should make every effort to involve you in your child's education and professionals have specific legal obligations to involve you in making decisions about your child's education, welfare and additional support (see section 5.3). Legal guidance (Additional Support for Learning Act Code of Practice) sets out what all professionals (i.e. not just education staff) are expected to do to make sure you can be involved. In all aspects of dealing with your child, staff should value the knowledge and experience you have of your child, acknowledge any information you give them, and respect your point of view. This does not mean that the professionals involved with your child will always agree with you and they will take decisions according to what they believe is in the best interest of your child. Staff should try to reach agreement with you and make every effort to avoid you having to go through the dispute resolution process or the Additional Support Needs Tribunal (see section 5.9 and 5.10). If you and staff disagree about what is in the best interests of your child you might find mediation useful (see section 5.7).

The legal guidance in the Additional Support for Learning Code of Practice says that staff should make sure you have all the information you need (for example that you are given all relevant papers well before meetings), that you understand the authority's procedures and know how you can access support if you want it. The information should be understandable and be written in clear, jargon-free language. You should be given the information you need automatically and be able to have it in different formats if necessary (for example Braille, audio or alternative languages). The education authority should also do its best to provide you with an interpreter if you need one.

Someone from the education authority should have responsibility for keeping you up to date (if your child has a CSP this may be the CSP co-ordinator, see section 3.5) and if you do not know who this is you can ask your child's head teacher or nursery manager. This person will be able to answer any questions you might have and respond to any concerns or problems (for example if the support that has been agreed is not delivered). They should also keep you informed at every stage about what to expect and what will happen next.

If your child has additional support needs (and particularly if they have a CSP) it is likely that the main way in which you will be involved in making decisions will be by attending meetings. Again, the Additional Support for Learning Code of Practice gives guidance to professionals about what is expected of them when there are meetings about your child's education:

- You should be asked what time and place suits you and any accessibility issues should be taken into account
- You should be sent papers well before the meeting and a note of the meeting shortly afterwards
- You should be given the chance to add points to the agenda, at the same time as everyone else
- Everyone at the meeting should be clear about what peoples' roles and responsibilities are in relation to your child and should have knowledge of your child's additional support needs
- There should be no 'hidden issues' or 'last minute surprises'

- Decisions should be made and agreed in the meeting, while you are there, and not afterwards (unless there are further discussions with you)
- Enough time should be allowed for meetings so that discussions are not rushed and decisions can be made properly.

5.2 Information

One of the key ways in which staff should support you to be involved and work in partnership with them is to make sure you have the information you need. Your child's school or nursery should have mechanisms in place to keep you informed about your individual child's progress (for example parents' nights) and about the school/nursery more widely (for example the school handbook or newsletter). By law you are entitled to receive 3 specific types of information:

- Basic information – this is intended to help you if you are considering asking for a place for your child in an alternative school (i.e. not the local school) and must include details of how the authority makes decisions about placing requests; arranges for children to start school early; and provides school meals, transport and boarding accommodation
- School information – this is available to you when your child is attending, or is about to start attending, a school and must include a range of information such as the school's contact details, policies, procedures, facilities, educational aims, and arrangements for providing meals, medical care, and organisation of the school day/terms
- Supplementary information – this is information that is not given to you automatically but which you can ask for, for example details of the education authority's policies and complaints systems.

Under the Freedom of Information (Scotland) Act 2002 you have the right to ask for and be given information from education authorities. This includes information on paper and on computer files such as e-mails. Your child also has this right if they have legal capacity (see section 1.7).

Examples of things you might use Freedom of Information to get are:

- The school's anti-bullying policy (or any other policy held by the school or education authority)
- Minutes of any education authority meetings, including those with outside agencies
- E-mails sent by members of staff.

Some information will already be published, as part of the education authorities' publication scheme. The publication scheme is a published document that shows:

- The information they already make available or intend to make available
- Where you can find the information
- Whether it is available free of charge or for a fee (from Your Right to Know, Scottish Information Commissioner/Scottish Consumer Council, 2005).

Making a Freedom of Information Request

- You must put your request in writing or any other form that can be kept for future use, such as e-mail, fax, audio or video tape
- You do not have to say you are using your rights under freedom of information or give any reasons for asking
- You can ask anyone from a receptionist to a senior official for the information
- If you do not provide enough detail to allow the authority to identify the information, or if your request is unclear, the authority can ask you to supply more details. That may include asking you why you want the information. However, you do not have to tell the authority why you want it and if you choose not to give a reason you should not be treated any differently.

Taken from of Your Right To Know (Scottish Information Commissioner/ Scottish Consumer Council, 2005)

The education authority should reply to your request for information as soon as possible but must reply within 20 working days. For more information on Freedom of Information contact the Scottish Information Commissioner for a copy of Your Right to Know (Scottish Information Commissioner/SCC, 2005) which provides more details on the Act.

What information should the education authority give me about additional support needs?

By law there is specific information about additional support needs that education authorities must make available to you:

• Who within your education authority can give you more information and advice if your child has additional support needs (i.e. the education authority contact person, see section 1.1)

• The authority's policy in relation to additional support needs

• How the authority identifies which children and young people have additional support needs and which need a CSP

• How the authority will make sure it is meeting the needs of children with additional support needs

• Independent mediation services, including details of how to make use of this service

• How the authority carries out reviews of CSPs

• How you (or your child if they are aged 16 or over) can ask for an assessment

• How the authority will involve you and your child (regardless of their age) in the additional support needs process

• What type of support is available for children with additional support needs

• What you can do if a problem arises or you disagree with the authority

• Other organisations which can give you further support, information or advice (e.g. speech and language therapy services, social work services, voluntary organisations or advocacy services).

This information might be on your local council's website or you can ask for it either from your child's school or nursery or by getting in touch with the education authority contact person (see section 1.1). The information should be available in other languages and alternative formats including audio tape, Braille and sign language.

While you can ask for this information at any time there are particular situations in which the education authority must, by law, provide it to you automatically. If your child has additional support needs you have the right to be given advice and information and if your child is assessed and found to have additional support needs the authority must provide you with the name and contact details of the person who can give you this. You will probably get a lot of information directly from the school or nursery but if this does not happen or you would like further information or advice you should contact this person.

What information do professionals have about my child and how can I see it?

The school and education authority will keep records on your child. These might be progress records, personal learning plans or other records about the education your child receives. Education records may include information on attainment, health information and information on assessments carried out.

Your child will also have health records which have information about your child's physical and mental health. These records are created by health professionals, including general practitioners (GPs), hospital doctors, nurses, dentists, health visitors, occupational therapists, physiotherapists, speech therapists and many others.

In some cases there will also be social work records held by the social work department at the local authority.

Education, health and social work records all have personal information about your child and your family. Because of this, there is a Data Protection Act (1998) which means that you can see any of this information. Your child also has this right if they have legal capacity (see section 1.7). There are some types of information that you might not be able to see. Sometimes this might mean withholding a whole document or it might mean blacking out the information so you cannot see it (see box).

What information might be withheld?

Some information may be withheld from you. This includes information that:

- could cause serious harm to you or another person's physical or mental health
- could identify someone else – for example another pupil (but not teachers) and that person has not consented to being identified
- forms part of a court report or a report made by or for a reporter to a children's panel
- would help to prevent or detect crime
- is in a reference concerning education, training or employment given by the education authority or school
- is about adoption records or reports
- is confidential because of legal privilege or was provided in the context of a lawyer-client relationship
- the education authority or school has a legal obligation not to disclose.

Taken from What's On My Record? Scottish Consumer Council, 2001

In addition to your right to see the document itself, you are also entitled to see:

- a description of the personal information that is held in the record
- details of the purposes for which the information is processed
- details of the courses of information (if known)
- details of the individuals or organisations to whom information from the record might have been given.

To see the information held in your child's records, you should write (by post or e-mail) to the organisation that you think holds the information, for example the education authority, health board or social work department. There may be a Data Protection Officer who is employed to deal with these information requests and you might want to telephone the agency to ask them who to send the request to. Some agencies may also have a form for you to fill out which might be easier than writing a letter. Because it is personal information, the agency might ask you to prove that you are who you say you are and they may also ask for more information to help them find your records.

You can be charged a fee of up to £10 to see your social work records and up to £50 to see your health records. If you want to see your child's education records then the prices are slightly different, you could be charged up to a maximum of:

- £1 for up to 19 pages
- £9 for up to 99 pages
- £10 for up to 149 pages
- £50 for 500 pages or more.

Some agencies do not charge people to see the records, but you should be aware that they can charge you if they want to. The agency must send you a copy or arrange for you to inspect their copy within 40 days of receiving your request.

If any information on your child's record is wrong or misleading you can have it corrected or removed. This includes any opinions recorded which were based on inaccurate information. If the agency holding the record does not agree to change it, you can complain to the U.K. Information Commissioner who can order them to change or remove incorrect information. You can contact the U.K. Information Commissioner for advice on any aspect of information and records about your child and can complain to the Commissioner if you are unhappy with how your request to see the information was handled (see section 7.6 for contacts).

Information held in co-ordinated support plans

If your child has a co-ordinated support plan, the law says that the education authority must give you a copy of it. You can also inspect the education authority's copy of the plan. Because this is covered by the Additional Support for Learning Act, you do not need to use the Data Protection Act to see a copy of it. The CSP is a confidential document and in general the education authority should get your consent before showing it to anyone. The authority can show it to Her Majesty's Inspectorate of Education (HMIe), Scottish Ministers (when they are considering a Section 70 appeal, see section 5.11), the Principal Reporter, the CSP co-ordinator, and those the authority think need to see it in the best interests of your child (for example, those providing your child's support) without your consent, but they should always seek consent first.

Sharing information and confidentiality

To make sure that your child gets the best possible support, tailored to their needs, some of the professionals that work with you and your family will have to share information. For example, information might be shared between the school and a further education college to plan for your child's support once they leave school, or a speech therapist might share information with the school to help the teachers understand and support your child's needs.

The Data Protection Act 1998 is based on several principles, including that personal data should not be passed on without your permission, but this is not always the case.

The NHS is required by law to keep personal health information stored about you and your child confidential. That means that they cannot give the education authority or social work department information without your permission unless there are exceptional circumstances, for example child protection issues, or if it would harm you or others not to tell the other professionals.

The school and education authority should respect your right to confidentiality over health issues. They can request personal information on your child's health if they need to protect other people from harm, for example if your child had an infectious disease or if they were a danger to themselves and others.

If someone asks for your permission to share information they should tell you what your information will be used for and what your consent means in practice, for example, who will see the information and whether they will pass it on to anyone else.

5.3 When do I have a specific legal right to be involved?

While professionals should enable you to be involved generally in your child's education, welfare and support, there are particular times when the law gives you explicit rights to be involved. By law the education authority must ask for your views and take them into account when:

- It is assessing your child for additional support needs
- Deciding what support to put in place for your child
- Planning for your child leaving school
- Planning for a change in your child's education (for example moving schools or starting primary school).

In some situations the authority must ask both you and your child for your views:

- Deciding whether your child needs a CSP
- Preparing a CSP
- Reviewing a CSP.

When your child reaches 16 the right to have views asked for and taken into account in these situations lies with them (i.e. the authority are not legally obliged to ask you for your views) unless they do not have sufficient understanding (i.e. they lack legal capacity, see section 1.7) in which case you would have the right on their behalf. In reality most parents will still play an important part in their child's education and support even when they are 16 or over and, where your child has no objections, you should not be stopped from being involved.

5.4 What school level issues can I comment on?

The law also gives you rights to be involved in a number of school-wide issues. One of these is the 'school development plan' that your child's school has to produce each year setting out annual targets along with how it plans to improve standards. School development plans often include information about how the school will improve access for pupils with additional support needs and the local council's 'accessibility strategy' will inform this. The accessibility strategy is a plan that the local council has to produce every three years showing how it will improve access to education for disabled pupils. The strategy must cover three main areas: improving access to the curriculum; improving physical access; and improving access to information normally provided in writing.

You have the right to comment on both the school development plan and the local authority's accessibility strategy. The law says that parents (and pupils) must be consulted on both of these plans so you could be contacted and asked to take part in this. The law however does not oblige the school or council to consult with every parent so you might not receive information about how to be involved. If you are not aware of consultation on the school development plan or accessibility strategy you can contact the school or council (education department) and ask to see a copy of the plan and be informed of when it will be reviewed and how you can be involved.

5.5 How will my child be involved?

Your child has the legal right to be involved in decisions that significantly affect them. There are particular times during the process of planning their additional support when they must be asked for their views and have these taken seriously. This could happen fairly informally through the school or nursery staffs' day to day contact with your child and you should expect the school or nursery to try to create an environment where participation and decision-making are part of your child's everyday learning experience. At other times it could be necessary to ask for your child's view in a more formal way and this might involve them attending a meeting (this is likely to be a CSP meeting, see section 3.5) with you and those who are planning their additional support. If this happens you your child should be fully informed about the purpose of the meeting and what will be discussed and should have a genuine opportunity to speak and be listened to. The school should make it as easy as possible for your child to get their views across and the Additional Support for Learning Code of Practice gives advice to professionals on how they can do this (see box).

A child or young person may benefit from:

- being given enough time to prepare and to go over the ideas and material to be discussed
- being given information in a form they can understand
- a teacher or other helper to help understand the meaning of key terms and concepts
- a supportive communication facilitator to tease out the full meaning of all of the issues
- specialised or new vocabulary (perhaps in sign or symbol form) in order to discuss a particular topic
- support to go over ideas, perhaps on several occasions
- help to understand outcomes and agreements.

Issues related to language

- if spoken English is not the child's or young person's first language, consider using an interpreter
- consider using a facilitator for those with language or speech difficulties
- use appropriate alternative or augmentative communication systems such as visual aids and/or sign language for deaf and/or communication impaired children or young people
- take account of any cultural preferences
- take time to explain what decision has to be made, why it's important and how the child or young person can influence it.

Taken from the Additional Support for Learning Code of Practice.

There may be factors that make it more difficult for your child to communicate or express him/herself, for example communication difficulties or behavioural problems. The education authority is still required by law to ask their views and should only ask for yours instead of your child's if your child is entirely unable to express an opinion. The law clearly states that your child should not be denied the opportunity to express their view because of a lack of the support they need to communicate. The authority should take advice from you and other professionals about how best to communicate with your child and should do so in a way that suits them. For example this could be through an interpreter if their first language is not English, using an electronic communication aid, or could be done by recording their views in writing or on video before a meeting.

Once the authority has noted your child's view (it should always be noted in the CSP) they will decide how much weight to give it. When the authority is deciding this it will take into account your child's:

• level of understanding

• ability to express their views

• understanding of all the options available, and

• how well the person recording the views knows your child.

The law gives you the right to act on behalf of your child if they 'lack capacity' (see section 1.7). The education authority will decide whether your child lacks capacity and should discuss this with you and all other relevant professionals (for example others who work with your child on a daily basis). If communication issues mean there is doubt about your child's level of understanding a speech and language assessment should be done. Legal guidance says that the authority, you, and others who know your child should try to reach agreement about whether or not your child has capacity. The reason for the final decision should be written down and if you or your child do not agree with the decision this should also be recorded.

5.6 Can I access support or advocacy?

At times when your child needs extra support with learning you might find that you have more contact with their school or nursery than usual. This can be made easier by having someone who can support you, for example by going with you to meetings or by acting on your behalf. You have the right to take a 'supporter' with you to any meetings with the school, nursery or authority about your child's additional support needs (although the education authority does not have to pay for this). This can be anyone including a friend, relative, befriender, someone from a voluntary organisation, or a professional you have contact with (as long there is not a conflict of interest, for example if they would have to attend meetings in their professional capacity they might not be able to also act as your supporter).

The Additional Support for Learning Act Code of Practice describes the kind of ways in which a supporter might help:

• Acting as a sounding board in preparing for the meeting

• Taking notes so that you can participate more fully in the discussions

• Suggesting points for further clarification, questions to ask or giving you advice during the meeting.

An advocate has a similar role to a supporter but will also act on your behalf in some or all of your dealings with the education authority. An advocate can speak on your behalf at meetings and can write to or phone the authority for you. An advocate might give you advice but their job is to represent your views, so regardless of whether or not they agree with those views they must argue your case. There are a number of organisations that offer professional advocacy and the Additional Support for Learning Code of Practice lists others who can act as an advocate:

• Someone who has already been acting as a supporter and that you want to act on your behalf

• Someone who is not trained in advocacy but who has relevant expertise, for example they might have knowledge about education law or about your child's additional support needs

- A voluntary organisation (this does not have to be an organisation which specialises in advocacy).

You can use a supporter or advocate at any time and it can be helpful if you are anxious about approaching your child's school, nursery or the education authority or about attending meetings. A supporter or advocate can also help if you disagree with the education authority or if the relationship has become difficult. It might simply be useful to have someone who can take notes at meetings, allowing you to concentrate fully on the discussions, and can give you a second opinion and discuss your child's educational needs with you.

The education authority can only prevent you from using a supporter or an advocate if they consider your request to do so as 'unreasonable'. The law does not give a concrete definition of 'unreasonable' but it gives the example that if the authority is concerned that the supporter or advocate is unable to represent you 'appropriately' then it can refuse your request to have the supporter or advocate present.

> **Finding out more about advocacy and supporters**
>
> The education authority contact person (see section 1.1) will be able to give you more information about supporters and advocacy services.

5.7 Mediation

You have a right to independent mediation services and the local authority must provide these to help avoid, or resolve, disputes about all aspects of the additional support needs system. You can use mediation at any stage and it is meant to help to prevent a breakdown of the relationship between you and the authority. The school, nursery or education authority might suggest using mediation and it is your choice to use it or not. Choosing to use mediation does not affect your rights to use formal complaint routes including dispute resolution and the Additional Support Needs Tribunal.

If you decide to try mediation the mediator will facilitate discussion between you and the authority and try to help you to reach an agreement on the best way forward. The mediator will be entirely impartial and will not make any decisions or take sides in the disagreement. Parents and professionals often find that mediation can do a lot to improve communication, rebuild relationships and help avoid conflicts.

The law says that the mediation service your local authority provides must be independent. Some authorities may use an independent mediation organisation or a free-lance mediator but the authority can also use its own mediation services. The service is considered to be 'independent' as long as the mediator is not involved with the authority's additional support needs system (except in the role of independent mediator). The mediator could also come from another local authority. The Additional Support for Learning Act Code of Practice says that however the authority chooses to provide the mediation service it must be objective and impartial and both you and the authority must be satisfied that the mediator is independent.

It is the authority's responsibility to arrange mediation sessions and to ensure they can take place at a neutral venue, for example you may prefer not to meet in the education authority offices or in the school.

If the education authority is not responsible for your child's education (for example if they are home educated or attend an independent or grant-aided school paid for privately) you have the right to independent mediation if the authority refuses to respond to a request from you to assess whether your child has additional support needs or whether they meet the criteria for a CSP.

Case studies

Andrew is in primary 3 and is making much faster progress than his classmates. He is starting to get bored at school and is not being challenged by the work he is set. Andrew's parents have discussions with the school about how to make sure he is getting the most out of his education but find it hard to agree on the best course of action. The relationship between the school and Andrew's parents becomes increasingly difficult and Andrew's parents are worried that his education will suffer. They decide to try mediation and contact the education authority to find out how to go about this. Mediation sessions are set up and this helps improve the communication between Andrew's parents and the school and to begin to look at the best way forward.

Stacey is 16 and receives support at school because she suffers from depression and anxiety. When she goes into 5th year she becomes stressed about her exams and about leaving school and her depression and anxiety become far worse. Stacey talks to her teacher about increasing the support she receives but the Head Teacher feels the school is not able to provide more support. Stacey talks to her parents who also contact the school and are told that no more support is available. Stacey and her parents then contact the education authority but feel that they are not being properly listened to so decide to refer their case to dispute resolution (see section 5.9). The education authority suggests mediation and Stacey and her parents agree. Mediation sessions are arranged and Stacey, her parents, the Head Teacher and someone from the education authority discuss the situation. After talking with the help of a mediator it becomes clear that there have been some misunderstandings on both sides. Once these issues have been aired and everyone has been given the chance to explain their points of view, communication began to improve and an agreement was reached.

5. 8 How do I make a complaint?

In an ideal world your child's additional support will be arranged successfully through ongoing discussion and good communication between you and the school. However sometimes problems can come up and you might disagree with the school or be unhappy with the way in which they are dealing with your child's needs. Most complaints are dealt with at the level of the individual school or nursery and in the first instance you should talk to a member of staff from your child's school or nursery. This could be their class teacher, learning support teacher or you might wish to contact the teacher in charge of their year or the head teacher. The relevant staff will then discuss the issue with you and your child and try to come to an agreement. You can use a supporter or advocate to support you in contacting the school or nursery and to take part in these discussions (see section 5.6).

The school or nursery will have a procedure for dealing with problems or complaints and will be able to give you details of this, including named contacts at each stage. The complaints system should be designed to try to deal with problems at the earliest stage possible and stop the relationship between you and the school/nursery from being damaged. If you have a concern you should not hesitate to contact the school or nursery at an early stage and this can help prevent reaching the stage of making a formal complaint or appealing to the dispute resolution process or Additional Support Needs Tribunal (see section 5.10).

If the problem is not resolved through discussions with the school or nursery then you can involve the education authority. The education authority will also have a complaints procedure and must have information on this up-to-date and available to you. You can ask for information about how to make a complaint by contacting the education department of your local council and it is often also available on the council's website. Some authorities have a telephone helpline for dealing with complaints and you should also be able to complain in writing or in person. The education authority should allocate a named officer to investigate your complaint, reach a decision and give you information about mediation services and possible next steps.

If you are unhappy with the decision of the education authority officer then you can take your complaint to either the local authority's dispute resolution system or to an Additional Support Needs Tribunal (see section 5.10). These are solely for complaints about additional support needs and do not deal with general education complaints. The Additional Support Needs Tribunal deals only with issues related to Co-ordinated Support Plans (CSPs) and the dispute resolution system acts on complaints relating to additional support needs but not to CSPs. Generally the dispute resolution process is the option available to you if your child has additional support needs but does not have a CSP.

5.9 Dispute resolution

The law requires all local authorities to have mechanisms in place to refer complaints to 'dispute resolution' (also known as 'independent external adjudication') to deal with disagreements relating to additional support needs. Dispute resolution deals with complaints relating to additional support needs but which cannot be taken to an Additional Support Needs Tribunal (see section 5.10) or the education authority Appeal Committee (see section 4.4). You can use it to appeal:

• disagreements relating to assessments (see section 2.4)

• the provision being given to your child (including equipment and auxiliary support)

• support being given from outwith the education authority

• failure of the authority to provide the support agreed in your child's CSP (this is the only issue in relation to a CSP that you can refer to dispute resolution).

The law on dispute resolution had not been finalised at the time of writing so this may not be a definitive list of what you can use it to appeal. If you have a disagreement that you cannot take to an Additional Support Needs Tribunal or the education authority

Appeal Committee and it is not listed above, we recommend that you contact Enquire (see section 7.6 for contacts) for advice. You can also ask your education authority contact person (see section 1.1) for information about the dispute resolution system in your area. If you make a complaint to dispute resolution the authority must acknowledge this and Scottish Ministers will then decide whether your case can be taken forward.

What does dispute resolution involve?

Dispute resolution is where an independent third party (who is external to the local authority) looks objectively at all the details of your case and makes a decision on the best way forward; this is called 'independent external adjudication'. The independent adjudicator will come from a national pool of adjudicators run by the Scottish Executive. The adjudicator will go over all the details of the disagreement by reviewing all the paper records (the education authority will be expected to have these ready and provide them to the adjudicator) and can ask for further information from you or the authority if necessary. You can also provide the adjudicator with additional information and the education authority must automatically tell you how to do this and what support is available to help you. Once the adjudicator has reached a decision a letter will be sent to both you and the authority with details of the decision and recommendations of what should happen next. There is no legal obligation to accept the decision and recommendations but legal guidance is clear that they should be accepted and acted upon in the vast majority of cases.

The process of independent external adjudication should take a maximum of eight weeks from when you made your complaint. Your case could take longer but only with good reason, for example if the referral was made close to the school holidays this may delay the process.

5.10 Additional Support Needs Tribunals

The Additional Support Needs Tribunals are completely independent of local authorities and national government. They are overseen by a national president (you can find out who this is by looking on the Additional Support Needs Tribunals website at www.asntscotland.gov.uk) who is accountable to the Scottish Committee of the Council on Tribunals (see section 7.6 for contacts). Tribunals generally deal with issues relating to co-ordinated support plans and have the power to instruct an education authority and to set a timescale for the authority to comply with its decision. The education authority must, by law, do what the tribunal decides. The tribunal can also force an authority to provide certain pieces of information and can summon witnesses to attend hearings.

The Additional Support Needs Tribunals have produced information for parents and young people about the tribunal process (see section 7.6 for contacts).

What can I refer to a tribunal?

If you have a complaint in relation to a Co-ordinated Support Plan that has not been resolved through the school, nursery or education authority complaints procedures you can refer it to an Additional Support Needs Tribunal. The issues you can take to a tribunal are:

The education authority's decision:

• to prepare a CSP

• not to prepare a CSP

• to continue a CSP (after a CSP review)

• not to continue a CSP (after a CSP review)

• to refuse your request to review a CSP earlier than the regular 12 month review timescale

• to refuse your request to assess your child for a CSP

A failure on the part of the education authority to:

• prepare a CSP within the 16 week time limit

• review a CSP within 12 months of it being prepared

• complete a CSP review within the 12 week timescale

Other issues you can appeal are:

- the contents of a CSP
- the refusal of a placing request (this applies if your child has a CSP, is waiting for one to be prepared, or has been refused one and this has been referred to a tribunal).

How do I appeal to a tribunal?

If you are considering making an appeal to an Additional Support Needs Tribunal (this is often called 'making a reference') you can get advice and information about how to do this from the Additional Support Needs Tribunal itself (for contacts see section 7.6) and the officer responsible for providing advice and information about additional support needs within your education authority will be able to give you contacts for other sources of support, advice and information (for example local or national voluntary organisations).

If you decide to make a reference you will have to contact the tribunal (for contacts see section 7.6) who will send you a form to fill in (you can also access and fill in this form on the tribunals' website at www.asntscotland.gov.uk). The form will ask you to explain the reasons for making the reference and to enclose photocopies of certain relevant documents (see box). If you do not send all of the information the tribunal needs it will write to you and usually you will have 10 working days to provide them with the information.

Guidance on the Additional Support Needs Tribunals gives suggestions on the information you could include:

- why you think your child is not making progress
- why you think your child needs extra support
- what sort of help you think your child needs
- if your child has a CSP, what changes you would like made to it
- if you are appealing a refused placing request, why you think your child should go to the particular school/nursery

The documents you should include are photocopies of:

- the letter containing the decision you are appealing
- your child's CSP if they have one
- all papers attached to the CSP.

If you are appealing a placing request you must also give full details of this including the name, address and postcode of the school you want your child to attend. You must also have made sure that there are places available at that school and inform the school that you have asked that it be the named school in your child's CSP (see section 3.5 for more on CSPs and section 4.4 for placing requests). You will have to tell the tribunal you have done all of this when you make your reference.

If you have a supporter, advocate (see section 5.6), or solicitor they can act as a representative and make the reference to the tribunal on your behalf. If someone makes the reference on your behalf you will still have to sign the form or attach an accompanying letter (signed by you) stating that this person is acting on your behalf. You can also ask that paperwork be sent to your representative by including their contact details on the reference form. If you do this then papers will only be sent to your representative and not directly to you.

If English is not your first language you can make your reference in your own language and it will be translated by the tribunal.

What happens once I have made a reference?

Once the tribunal has received your completed reference form it will make an initial decision about whether your appeal falls within its remit. If your complaint does not seem to be within the Additional Support Needs Tribunals' remit they will write to you and ask if you have further information that they can consider. If it is decided that the tribunals can deal with your case they will contact you and tell you that your reference has been 'registered'. At this stage you will be given an idea of when your hearing will be and be asked when would suit you and any witnesses you have.

Once your reference has been registered you will have the chance to prepare a 'case statement' and the tribunal will send you information and guidance about how to do this (you will have 30 working days to do this). You do not have to have a case statement but it is an opportunity to provide the tribunal with any information that was not on your original reference form. You can give information in writing, by attaching reports, or in video or audio formats (if you are using video or audio you should send 5 copies to the tribunal, this is one for the two tribunal members, convenor, education authority, and tribunal administration). If there is a particular piece of information you want to include but it is held by the education authority and the authority refuse to give it to you, you can contact the tribunal which has the power to force the authority to release the information (see also section 5.2 for your rights to information).

Before the hearing you will be sent a copy of the education authority's case statement and a copy of yours will be sent to the authority. There will be a chance at the hearing (but not before) to make comments or ask questions about the case statements.

If a document is not available within the 30 days you have to prepare your case statement you can send it later but it must reach the tribunal and the education authority at least 5 working days before the hearing. You can also take information with you to the hearing only if it was not available earlier (in which case you will need to take 5 copies).

What happens at a tribunal hearing?

The tribunals are designed to be as family-friendly and informal as possible. Those likely to be present at a tribunal hearing are:

• The tribunal convenor and two panel members who will hear your case
• You and/or your child's other parent
• Your child (the tribunal will want to know your child's views, however whether or not your child attends the hearing will depend on whether you and your son/daughter feel this is appropriate)

- A member of staff from the education authority (and possibly a colleague who will attend but not participate in the hearing)
- Up to two witnesses to speak in your support
- Up to two witnesses to speak in support of the education authority
- Your supporter if you have one (see section 5.6) (who can attend but not participate in the hearing)
- A member of the tribunal administrative staff who will meet you and the education authority staff, show you where to go, and explain what will happen, and give you any help you may need
- An interpreter or signer if this is needed
- Possibly an observer from the Scottish Committee of the Council on Tribunals or someone being trained by the tribunal.

Supporters, advocates and legal representation at a tribunal hearing

The Additional Support Needs Tribunals are set up to be less formal than a court. However you may want to take a supporter who can sit with you during the hearing but cannot take part (this could be a friend or relative for example). If you would like more assistance than this you can take an advocate who can participate in the hearing, including speaking on your behalf. Finally you can take a solicitor (as can the education authority) but the tribunals try to discourage this to avoid the hearings becoming more formal and court-like.

For more information on supporters and advocates see section 5.6. The Additional Support Needs Tribunals (contacts in section 7.6) will be able to advise you further on who you can bring to a tribunal hearing.

When you arrive at a hearing you will be met by a member of tribunal administrative staff who will explain what is going to happen and answer any questions you have. The hearing will normally be scheduled to last around half a day (it is possible, but unlikely, that the convenor will decide a second hearing needs to take place) and will normally take place around a table. The convenor will begin by explaining how the hearing will work. You will not be expected to make one statement on the whole of your case. Instead each issue will be dealt with one at a time and the convenor will try to make sure everyone is able to fully explain their point of view. The convenor and panel members should not use jargon or unnecessarily technical language and if there is anything you do not understand you should feel free to ask. Through asking questions of you, the member of education authority staff, and any witnesses, the panel members will try to establish the facts, what the outcome of the hearing should be, and what the best course of action is for your child. You and the education authority will also be able to ask questions of witnesses (both your own and each others) throughout the hearing. You will also have a chance at the end of the hearing to add any additional points.

The hearing should normally be held no more than two hours travel time from where you live and will probably start at either 10am or 2pm. You will be able to reclaim travel costs for yourself, your child's other parent, your child, a friend or relative there to look after your child, your supporter, and your witnesses (it will generally be expected that you use public transport wherever possible). The tribunal will not provide childcare. If you have any specific requirements (for example if you need a signer or interpreter at the hearing) you should state this on your reference form and the tribunal will arrange and pay for this.

Timescales

Action	Timescale
Making your reference	2 months from the date of the decision or failure that you are appealing (if you make a reference later than this without giving reasons the tribunal will write and ask you to explain so that they can still consider accepting your appeal)
Tribunal contacting you to say: • Whether or not it can deal with your case • More information is needed (you will normally have 10 working days to provide this)	Within 10 working days of you making your reference
Time allowed to prepare your case statement (from tribunal registering your reference, i.e. accepting your case)	30 working days
Notice given of hearing date	Minimum of 10 working days
Tribunal decision	Within 10 working days of hearing

5.11 Other mechanisms for sorting out problems

The system for resolving disputes put in place by the Additional Support for Learning Act has been designed to try to resolve problems quickly and easily. However, if you have been through mediation, dispute resolution or an additional support needs tribunal and are still unhappy about how your complaint has been dealt with by the education authority, there are other mechanisms for getting your complaint heard:

- The Public Services Ombudsman
- Scottish Ministers
- Sheriff Court
- Court of Session.

The process you have already been through and the type of complaint affects the body you should take your complaint to. The Additional Support for Learning Code of Practice sets out the different routes for dealing with disagreements or complaints. The chart below is a slightly simplified version of these routes.

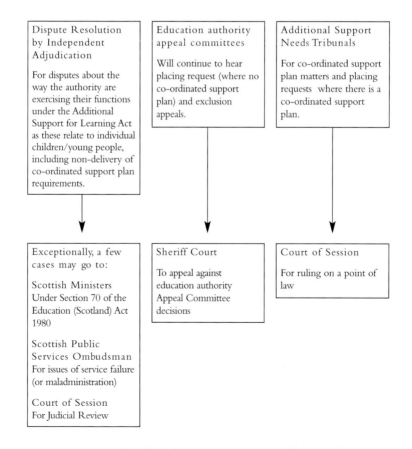

Dispute Resolution by Independent Adjudication

For disputes about the way the authority are exercising their functions under the Additional Support for Learning Act as these relate to individual children/young people, including non-delivery of co-ordinated support plan requirements.

Education authority appeal committees

Will continue to hear placing request (where no co-ordinated support plan) and exclusion appeals.

Additional Support Needs Tribunals

For co-ordinated support plan matters and placing requests where there is a co-ordinated support plan.

Exceptionally, a few cases may go to:

Scottish Ministers Under Section 70 of the Education (Scotland) Act 1980

Scottish Public Services Ombudsman For issues of service failure (or maladministration)

Court of Session For Judicial Review

Sheriff Court

To appeal against education authority Appeal Committee decisions

Court of Session

For ruling on a point of law

This section gives basic information about the bodies.

Scottish Public Services Ombudsman

The Scottish Public Services Ombudsman can investigate complaints where injustice or hardship has been caused to a member of the public through:

• Failure to provide a service that by law the authority has to provide
• Failure in a service provided
• Maladministration.

Service failure applies where the education authority has failed to provide a service that by law they have to provide. The Additional Support for Learning Act includes many services that by law the education authority has to provide. Throughout this handbook we have referred to things that the education authority must do and if they have not carried out these tasks then you can complain to the Public Services Ombudsman. If the education authority has not done something that the guidance says it should do, then this is something that the education authority has discretion over and you cannot take this complaint to the Ombudsman.

There may also be failure in a service provided – which means that the education authority did provide the service but it had serious shortcomings and problems. If you think that this has happened you can complain to the Ombudsman.

Maladministration means that the education authority has managed your child's case badly or improperly. The commonly used definition of maladministration gives the following examples:

'bias, neglect, inattention, delay, incompetence, ineptitude, perversity, turpitude and arbitrariness and so on'.

Additional examples of maladministration were quoted in the UK Parliamentary Ombudsman's annual report for 1993; including:

• rudeness (although that is a matter of degree)
• unwilling to treat someone as a person with rights
• refusal to answer reasonable questions

- not telling someone about their rights or entitlements when they have asked
- knowingly giving advice which is misleading or inadequate
- showing bias because of colour, sex, or any other grounds
- refusal to inform someone adequately of the right of appeal
- cavalier disregard of guidance which is intended to be followed in the interest of equitable treatment of those who use a service.

The Ombudsman cannot take on your case if it relates to a decision that the education authority made properly (for example, by following all their procedures), even if you disagree with the decision itself. They are also not able to deal with:

- Most personnel and commercial issues
- UK government departments
- Generally, matters which could be taken to court or a tribunal (including the Additional Support Needs Tribunals)
- Generally, things that happened more than 12 months ago.

Because the definitions of service failure and maladministration are complicated, the staff at the Scottish Public Services Ombudsman can help you to work out whether or not you can complain to the Ombudsman. You can contact the Ombudsman's office by telephone or arrange for a visit to their offices if you would prefer to discuss your complaint face to face.

If your complaint is found to be justified (in whole or in part) the report from the Ombudsman will contain recommendations for action. These recommendations will aim

- To put you in the position you would have been in if things had not gone wrong.
- To prevent the same thing happening to anyone else in future.

The Ombudsman will check that the agency you are complaining about has done what it said it would, or has acted on the recommendations. If it has not done so, they have the powers to present a special report to Parliament.

The contact details for the Public Services Ombudsman can be found in section 7.6.

Scottish Ministers

Under Section 70 of the Education (Scotland) Act 1980, Scottish Ministers can make education authorities (or any other body that has legal duties in relation to education) carry out their legal responsibilities.

If you think that the education authority, social work department or health board has failed to do something that the law says they must do in relation to your child's education you can bring it to the attention of the Minister for Education and Young People by writing to him/her at the Scottish Executive (see contacts section for the address). The Scottish Executive website (www.scotland.gov.uk) will tell you who the current Minister is.

If the Ministers agree that the agency has failed to carry out their legal responsibilities they will order the education authority or other agency to carry out their responsibilities. If they still don't provide the service the Ministers may make arrangements to provide the service in an alternative way and charge the agency that has failed to carry out its responsibilities.

Scottish Ministers can also consider appeals in relation to Sex, Race and Disability Discrimination by education providers (see section 6.1 for more information on equalities law). Ministers' decisions are open to Judicial Review through the Courts.

Sheriff Court

The Sheriff Court is a local court that deals with both civil and criminal procedures. You can appeal to the Sheriff Court about decisions made by the Education Authority Appeal Committee. There is a Sheriff Court in every city and most towns. The Sheriff will hear your case in the Sheriff Court of the district (there are 49 sheriff-court districts in Scotland). Juries are not used in civil court cases (any case about an education authority decision would be a civil case).

You should take legal advice if you are considering taking your case to the Sheriff Court; a solicitor will be able to advise you of how to do this.

Court of Sessions (Judicial Review)

Judicial Review is a way of challenging the decisions made by the education authority (or any other body). In Judicial Review a judge (or in some cases a panel of judges) will review your case and take evidence before deciding if the law was broken. If you want to go to Judicial Review you have to take your case to the Court of Sessions in Edinburgh.

You can start legal proceedings for Judicial Review if a public authority (which includes education authorities, local authorities and health boards):

• has done something that it does not have the legal power to do

• used its legal powers in a way that goes against the principles of the law (for example, if it did something that went against the principle of mainstream education)

• has failed to carry out its legal responsibilities.

If the Court of Sessions rules that the public authority has been acting illegally they can:

• make a declaration stating that a certain right exists

• order the public authority to stop doing something

• reverse the decision made by the authority

• award compensation for any damages caused.

Judicial Review is the final step in the complaints procedure and you should only consider it if all other attempts at reaching a solution (for example, mediation, alternative dispute resolution or the Tribunals) have failed. Going to court may take time, in some cases years, and the cost involved may be high. You may be eligible for Legal Aid to cover legal advice and representation. A solicitor will be able to advise you whether or not this is possible.

If you are thinking about going to court you should consult a solicitor who is familiar with education law (see section 7.6 for contacts).

Part 6:
Other issues

The previous sections of this handbook have covered most of the law which relates directly to additional support needs. However there are other, more general, issues that might affect your child.

6.1 Equalities legislation

The additional support needs system is closely related to laws designed to ensure that people are not discriminated against on any grounds. If your child has additional support needs they may also be protected by equalities legislation:

Disability Discrimination Act 1995 (DDA)

The DDA came into force in 1996 and was extended in 2002 (by the Special Educational Needs and Disability Act 2001) to cover education. The Act applies to all education providers including private schools. It also covers all early years settings whether they are providing education, care or a combination of both (this includes private nurseries, individual child minders and social work services).

The DDA defines disability as 'a physical or mental impairment, which has a substantial and long term adverse affect on a person's ability to carry out normal day-to-day activities'. So for example if your child has mobility problems, communication difficulties, mental health problems, or physical health issues they may have rights under the DDA. You can get more information about what the DDA covers and whether your child has a disability from the Disability Rights Commission (for contacts see section 7.6).

Definition of disability discrimination

There are two parts to the legal definition of disability discrimination:

1) Less favourable treatment

If your child's school or nursery treats them less favourably than other children for a reason relating to their disability this could be discrimination under the DDA. For example if your child was prevented from taking part in a particular class (such as a science practical) because they have behavioural difficulties related to autism this may be against the law. A school/nursery can treat your child less favourably if there is 'material and substantial' reason for doing this. However the school/nursery would be expected to have fully considered your child's needs and to have made 'reasonable adjustments' so that they can be treated equally to the other children. So in the example above it might be possible for the child to take part in the science practical with extra support, and if this was the case the school should provide this extra support (if they failed to do so this could be a 'failure to make reasonable adjustments' and could be a failure to provide for additional support needs under the Additional Support for Learning Act).

2) Failure to make reasonable adjustments

The DDA says that schools must make 'reasonable adjustments' to ensure that disabled children are not put at a disadvantage. This does not apply to making physical changes to the school (this is covered by the law on accessibility strategies, see below) or to providing auxiliary aids and services (your child has rights to these, if they need them, under the Additional Support for Learning Act). It does however require schools to make changes to its policies, procedures and practices, for example if your child had a hearing impairment you could expect the school to make adjustments such as training for teaching staff and ensuring that classrooms are set out in such a way as to ensure your child can see the teacher's face to lip read.

The DDA makes it illegal for an education authority to discriminate against your child for a reason that relates to their disability. This applies to all aspects of school and the law specifically refers to:

- admissions (for example decisions about a placing request)
- education (for example the curriculum)
- services related to education (for example school trips and school meals)
- exclusions.

If you think your child has been discriminated against for a reason which is connected to their disability you should first contact the Head Teacher (or equivalent person within your child's nursery or other early years service; this could be the nursery manager in a private nursery or the head teacher if it is a local authority nursery attached to a primary school). It may be that you and the Head Teacher are able to discuss what has happened and sort the problem out, for example it is possible that the Head Teacher has not known about your child being discriminated against and is able to deal with it and stop it from happening again. However if it cannot be solved at school level you can use the education authority's complaints system (see section 5.8). If the issue cannot be resolved by either the school or your education authority then you should get in touch with the Disability Rights Commission who can deal with your case in a number of ways including through their conciliation service or by helping you to take legal action (your child can also take legal action if they have legal capacity, see section 1.7). You or your child might also be entitled to Legal Aid to pay for a solicitor in this situation (see section 7.6 for contacts).

Accessibility strategies

All education authorities, independent schools and grant-aided schools must produce accessibility strategies every 3 years. These are plans which set out how access to education will be improved for disabled children and must cover:

- access to the curriculum
- physical access
- access to information normally provided in writing.

Accessibility strategies are not about individual children and young people but are aimed at removing barriers and making improvements that increase the overall level of accessibility of your child's school/nursery. The strategies must be based on the principle that disabled children and young people should:

- have access to a full and broad curriculum which is similar to that followed by non-disabled pupils
- be able to attend, wherever possible, the school of their choice and access all areas and activities of that school
- be provided with information in alternative formats and should have the same opportunities as non-disabled children and young people to give their views and communicate with school staff and other pupils.

You can ask to see a copy of your local authority's accessibility strategy (it may also be available on the authority's website) and the authority must give you a copy. If you do not believe that your child's school or pre-school is complying with the authority's accessibility strategy you can complain to the authority or to the Scottish Ministers (see section 5.8 on making a complaint and section 5.11 on complaining to ministers).

Race equality

The Race Relations Act 1976 and the Race Relations (Amendment) Act 2000 make it illegal for education authorities and independent schools to discriminate against your child on 'racial grounds'. Racial grounds means to discriminate because of colour, race, nationality or ethnic or national origins.

Definition of racial discrimination

Race discrimination can occur in two ways:

- Directly – treating a person on 'racial grounds' less favourably than other people in similar circumstances
- Indirectly – where a rule or condition which, on the face of it, applies to everyone actually affects one 'racial group' significantly more than others, to their detriment, and this cannot be justified by other (lawful) reasons.

Direct discrimination can take many forms. In a school setting this might include racist insults or comments, racially motivated harassment, or more subtle differences in marking or treatment. The education authority and schools must take reasonable steps to protect children from unlawful discrimination at school. If they fail to do so, then they can be held responsible for the discriminatory actions of others (e.g. a pupil, member of staff or a visitor to the school).

Indirect discrimination can sometimes be justified by other (lawful) reasons. In schools, there would have to be educational grounds for most (if not all) cases where justification is claimed. Any potential justification must outweigh the disadvantage suffered by the person(s) affected. For example, a school uniform rule insisting that boys wear caps was indirect discrimination, because it affected those who were required to wear turbans for cultural reasons. However, it would not be discrimination to ban Sikh ceremonial daggers, nor Scottish dirks, from school because this is justifiable on the grounds of safety.

It is unlawful for schools to discriminate on the grounds of race in any of the following areas:

- decisions or policies on admission
- access to educational benefits, grants, bursaries, facilities, or other services
- school meals, transport or uniform
- exclusions
- by subjecting pupils to any other disadvantage on racial grounds.

Taken from The A – Z Scots Education Law (SCC, 2004)

If you think your child has been discriminated against on racial grounds you should contact the Head Teacher (or equivalent person within an early years service) if possible and try to resolve it first at school level. If this does not work you can use the education authority's complaints procedure (see section 5.8). You can also take legal action through the Sheriff Court (the time limit for lodging your case is normally 6 months less one day from the date the discrimination occurred) and you can get help and advice with this from the Citizens Advice Bureau, the Commission for Racial Equality or a solicitor (for contacts see section 7.6).

Human rights

The Human Rights Act 1998 requires public authorities (including schools and education authorities) to adhere to the Convention for the Protection of Human Rights and Fundamental Freedoms (often called the European Convention on Human Rights or the Human Rights Convention). The convention sets out basic human rights, including the right to education, and the right not to be discriminated against in relation to any part of the convention. Decisions made by education authorities, schools, education appeals committees, children's hearings and courts must all conform to the Human Rights Convention.

Scottish legislation goes beyond the convention so if your child suffered discrimination in relation to their education it is more likely that you would challenge this under more specific laws such as the DDA. However if you believe your child's human rights have been breached you can take legal action under the Human Rights Act. For example issues such as school exclusions, religious education, school uniform and corporal punishment have all been challenged under human rights legislation.

You can contact the Scottish Human Rights Centre for further information about your rights under the European Convention and what steps you can take if you or your child's rights have been breached (see section 7.6 for contacts).

6.2 Equipment

If your child has additional support needs arising from a disability he/she may need specialised equipment in and/or out of school. The way in which equipment is provided will depend on what your child's needs are. Generally your child will be assessed by a professional (often a health professional) who will arrange for any necessary equipment to be provided. For example if your child has mobility difficulties they will be assessed by a physiotherapist and will probably be provided with equipment by the National Health Service.

If your child needs equipment specifically in relation to their learning then they could be entitled to this through the requirement on education authorities to meet additional support needs (see section 3.2 for more information).

6.3 Exclusion

In some circumstances the school might stop your child attending, either for a short period of time or permanently. This is called 'exclusion' but is sometimes also referred to as suspension, informal exclusion, cooling off period, sending a pupil home, permanent exclusion, or expulsion. All of these terms mean the same in law although some education authorities distinguish between 'temporary exclusion' (where your child is expected to return to the school) and 'removal from the register' (where your child would be removed from the school register and have to be educated elsewhere).

The school cannot simply send your child home, it must have a system in place for planning for exclusion and keeping you informed. While your child is excluded the education authority still has a legal responsibility to provide them with education (if they are of school age, generally 5-16) and may arrange to send them to another school.

Exclusion should only be used as a last resort and the education authority is only allowed to exclude your child where:

- you have not complied with the school rules or have stopped your child from complying with them, or have allowed your child to break them

- your child's continuing attendance at the school is likely to have a seriously detrimental affect on school order and discipline, or on the education of other pupils.

You or your child, if they have capacity (see section 1.7) can appeal against an exclusion by writing to the education authority appeal committee (see section 4.4).

6.4 Mainstream, special or residential schooling?

If your child has multiple or complex needs, the issue of whether or not to place them in a special school may come up. In general, the education system in Scotland is based on mainstreaming. That means that as far as possible children must be educated in the same primary or secondary school as their peers. However, mainstream schools may not be able to provide the level of care that some children with multiple or complex needs require.

Some mainstream schools now also have special units which can educate and support your child, either full-time or for part of the school week.

However, mainstream schools are not right for every child. In particular children who:

- require special facilities, teaching methods or expertise may receive better support in special schools
- have difficulty forming relationships with other, or may have severe behavioural difficulties, which can cause extreme disruption in mainstream schools and may affect the education of other children
- learn better in smaller classrooms with more one-to-one support which may not be possible in large mainstream schools.

Around 2 per cent of children in Scotland attend special schools. Special schools are likely to have staff who can support your child's medical, physical or social needs (for example educational psychologists or occupational therapists). The decision to educate your child in a special school may be taken before they start school, or you may make a placing request at any time (see section 4.4 for more information on making a placing request). In 2003/04, special schools accounted for 0.4 per cent of all placing requests (115 requests in total), of which 83 per cent were granted. Whenever the decision is being taken, you should be fully involved and you and your child's views should be taken into account by the education authority.

A small number of children in special schools attend on a residential basis so that they can receive full-time care. In 2004, a review by HMIe (the education inspectorate) found there were 34 residential schools in Scotland making provision for vulnerable children and young people:

- 23 catered for children and young people with additional support needs arising from significant social, emotional and behavioural difficulties. Most of the young people had been involved with Children's Hearings or experienced significant difficulties at mainstream schools

- 11 schools supported children and young people with a range of additional support needs, including sensory impairment, physical disabilities, autism and other complex needs. Some children had been placed primarily for care purposes, although they spent time with parents or carers at weekends and holidays (HMIe, 2005, Residential Care And Education: Improving Practice In Residential Special Schools In Scotland).

If you think your child might benefit from residential education, you should discuss it with your family's social worker, your child's head teacher or the education authority.

6.5 Medical attention at school

What if my child needs help with taking medicine at school?

Your school and education authority will have policies and procedures about what happens if your child needs help with taking medication at school. The education authority should have an agreement with the local Health Board and your child's individual school or nursery should cover this in its Health and

Safety policy. It may be that your child is helped by a non-health professional (for example their classroom teacher) and this person should be given the necessary medical training and support.

If your child needs medical assistance at school they should have a 'health care plan'. This should be drawn up with all the relevant health and education staff as well as with you and your child.

Consent to medical treatment

If your child has legal capacity (see section 1.7) they can give (or refuse) consent to medical treatment (including examinations) themselves. If your child does not have capacity it will generally be only people with parental rights who can give or refuse consent. The only exception to this is an emergency situation where someone who is over 16 and who has care and control of your child (but no parental rights or responsibilities), such as a grandparent, can consent to medical treatment. If this happens the person giving consent must have no reason to believe that you would have objected to your child receiving the medical treatment. The treatment must also have been reasonable to safeguard your child's health, development and welfare.

6.6 Moving and handling

If your child needs to be moved or lifted by school staff (for example in and out of a wheelchair) this should be done in a way that is safe and comfortable for your child and for staff. Health and safety law aims to protect your child when they are being moved and also prevent staff being injured by continuous moving or lifting. The law does not say that your child cannot be moved or lifted manually but it does say that this should be avoided if possible. This means that your child, particularly once they are older, will probably be lifted using equipment such as a hoist. The law also requires your child's school to carry out a 'risk assessment' in certain circumstances (for example a school trip or new activity). This involves identifying all potential moving and handling issues and weighing these up against the benefits of the trip or activity. A risk assessment may result in an activity being deemed too unsafe but the process should equally be about enabling your child to take part in activities by ensuring that moving and handling issues are well planned for in advance.

Case study

Craig is 16 and needs to use a hoist to get in and out of his wheelchair. His school is planning a trip to a local country park so they ask Craig's Occupational Therapist to carry out a risk assessment. The Occupational Therapist visits the country park and finds that most of the park is wheelchair accessible but that there are no hoists in the toilets and there is not space to bring a hoist from school. The Occupational Therapist talks to the Head Teacher and they weigh up the risk to staff of helping Craig manually in and out of his chair, the experience for Craig of being moved manually and the benefits of Craig going on the trip. They decide that given that Craig is not heavy for his age, can bear weight, and is likely to only need help in and out of his chair once during the trip that he can go. The Occupational Therapist talks to Craig about the trip and asks how he feels about the possibility of having to be helped manually. After some discussion Craig decides he would like to go on the trip even though he will not have access to a hoist.

6.7 Physical intervention / restraint

Physical punishment at school/nursery is illegal. Staff at your child's school are allowed to physically restrain your child, using reasonable force, if this is necessary to prevent an injury to your child, an injury to someone else, or damage to property. If your child's needs mean they need to be physically restrained then staff should be trained in how to do this safely. If your child is injured while being restrained you should seek legal advice. If the staff restraining your child were properly trained but used excessive force then they may be liable and face disciplinary proceedings. However if the staff were not trained then your child's school/nursery may be legally liable.

6.8 Safety and supervision

While your child is at school or nursery, the school/nursery has a legal responsibility to take 'reasonable care' of them. In primary school (if the school has 50 or more pupils) and in all special schools this includes providing supervision by at least one adult (aged 18 or over) during break times. It also means taking 'reasonable care' for the safety of your child (whatever stage or type of school they attend) in school, on school transport, on school trips, and at school events.

Although the school has responsibility for the safety and care of your child, the law also acknowledges that your child has some responsibility for their own actions. For example if your child was injured while under the care of their school then the school may not be to blame if it had taken all reasonable steps to avoid an accident and your child had behaved dangerously. However the law does say that the school must take into account the nature of individual children, so for example if your child had behavioural difficulties the school should take this into account in terms of safety and supervision.

The education authority is also responsible for making sure that school buildings meet safety requirements.

6.9 School holidays and support

Scottish schools must normally be open for at least 190 days a year, with the normal school year running from mid-August to late June or early July. The long summer holidays can be particularly stressful for all families and if your child has additional support needs you can face extra problems, for example with finding child care or leisure activities that can cater for your child's needs.

The law does not require education authorities to provide support or education in the school holidays. However, many now recognise the benefit of continuing to provide services.

You may find that the school offers summer playschemes or summer schools, some of which will be offered to children with specific additional support needs. While these are often provided for free, some authorities may charge for them because of the staff and accommodation costs associated with providing support in the holidays.

If you think your child would benefit from summer holiday activities, the school and education authority will be able to tell you what is on offer in your local area.

Alternatively, many voluntary organisations provide care and support in the summer holidays. Some of the organisations listed in the contacts section (7.6) may be able to help you to find summer holiday activities.

6.10 Transport

The education authority must provide free transport for your child to go to school and back if they are under 8 years old and live more than 2 miles away; or are 8 or over and live more than 3 miles away. This only applies if your child attends their local school, or another school nominated by the local authority (and not requested by you via a placing request).

Lack of suitable transport

Lack of suitable transport is listed as a potential reasonable excuse for non-attendance at school. This may apply where the route, though shorter than the statutory walking distance, is hazardous or otherwise unsuitable for children. In these circumstances, the education authority still has an obligation to provide education for a child. The simplest way of meeting this obligation is by providing free transport.

Taken from The A – Z Scots Education Law (SCC, 2004)

The education authority also has a responsibility to make sure that your child is safe on school transport. If your child has additional support needs, this may mean that they require assistance using school transport and the education authority should provide it as part of the additional support your child requires.

If your child goes to a special school, a residential school or another non-education authority school that you have made a successful placing request to, then the education authority must meet the transport costs of sending your child to that school. There may be a school bus or in other cases, perhaps because of small numbers of children attending the school, taxis may be provided. Whatever method of transport is put in place, the education authority must cover the full cost.

If you have successfully made a placing request for your child to be educated in a special school elsewhere in the UK or outwith the UK, then the education authority still has to cover the cost of transport to the school. The cost of this transport may well form part of their decision to allow placements outside of the UK.

Part 7:
Reference section

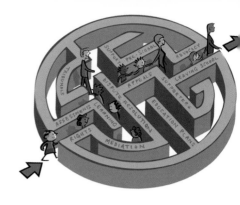

7.1 Glossary

Accessibility strategies – all education authorities have to produce accessibility strategies every 3 years which set out how access to education will be improved for disabled pupils.

Adaptations – altering buildings, equipment or furnishings to facilitate use by people who otherwise would have difficulty using them (for example, widening doors for wheelchair users).

Additional support – specialist support provided over and above what is generally provided by an education authority for children or young people of the same age in schools.

Additional support needs – your child has additional support needs if they need extra support (compared to their classmates) to get the most out of school and achieve their full potential.

Additional Support Needs Tribunals - the Tribunals make decisions on whether an education authority has carried out its duties under some parts of the Additional Support for Learning Act. They are completely independent of education authorities and the Scottish Executive and by law the education authority must do what the tribunal decides.

Adjudication – see Dispute Resolution.

Advocate – someone chosen by you to conduct discussions on your behalf with an education authority or to make representations to the authority.

Agencies – in this handbook, we use the word agencies to refer to the services that might support your child, for example education authorities, social work departments, health boards and the voluntary sector.

Assessment – an ongoing process of gathering, structuring and making sense of information about your child and their circumstances, in order to inform decisions about the actions necessary to maximise their potential.

Capacity – a legal term; if someone has capacity then they understand the decisions that they are making. Children are presumed to have capacity when they are 12 but a younger child may have enough understanding of the situation for it to be decided that they have capacity.

Care Plan – a plan of support written by the local authority for children who are looked-after. This may include information about their education needs.

Carer – includes parents and other people with parental responsibilities, public foster carers, relatives and friends who are caring for children under supervision requirements, and close relatives, such as siblings or grandparents caring for children who are not looked-after or are under home supervision requirements.

Child – a child is anyone under the age of 16.

Children's Hearing – a tribunal where three panel members decide whether or not a child needs supervision from the local authority (see looked-after children).

Civil proceedings – legal cases which deal with civil law, that is law which is not personal or criminal. All education law is civil law. The Sheriff Court (a local court) deals with most civil proceedings in Scotland.

Code of Practice ('the Code') – official guidance on the Additional Support for Learning Act. The Code has a legal status and education authorities, social work departments and health boards must 'have regard' to it.

Complex support need – for the purposes of a co-ordinated support plan, this is a need which has or is likely to have a significant adverse effect on the school education of the child or young person.

Conciliation – a type of dispute resolution used by the Disability Rights Commission. Conciliation involves an independent third party working with those in disagreement to help them resolve their dispute by listening to both sides and offering an opinion on how it should be settled. In conciliation, the two parties may not meet, and the conciliator will work with them separately, unlike in most mediation.

Co-ordinated support plan (CSP) – document to help plan the provision of services for children or young people whose additional support needs arise from complex, or multiple factors, which have a significant adverse effect on their school education and are likely to last at least a year, and which require support to be provided by an education authority and at least one other non-education service or agency.

Co-ordinated support plan co-ordinator – someone appointed by the education authority to co-ordinate the support your child receives, in line with their CSP.

Dispute resolution - the involvement of an independent, external adjudicator to examine the reasons for disagreement between parents, or a young person, and an education authority, over the exercise by the authority of any of its duties or functions under the Act, and to make recommendations for both parties aimed at resolving the dispute.

Disability - the definition of disability, set out in the Disability Discrimination Act 1995, is a physical or mental impairment, which has a substantial and long term adverse effect on a person's ability to carry out normal day-to-day activities.

Early years – a general term usually referring to children aged 0 – 3 years old, it can also be used as a description of services, for example early years care and education.

Education authority - in legal terms, education authority and local authority are the same thing. This book refers to an education authority when considering a local authority's educational functions, and to a local authority when referring to functions other than educational ones, such as social work services.

Education authority area – the geographical area which an education authority has responsibility for.

Education records – the official records held by education authorities on your child's education. These might include test results, exam results, health information or behaviour records.

Exclusion – when a school stops a child from attending, either for a short period of time or permanently, it is called 'exclusion'. It has to be carried out properly in accordance with the law; the school cannot just send your child home.

Flexi-schooling – where responsibility for a child's education is shared and they are educated at school part-time, and at home part-time.

Grant-aided school – a school in receipt of grant funding from the Scottish Executive. At present there are eight such schools.

Health Boards – the 15 NHS Boards in Scotland that deliver health services.

Home education – when children are educated at home, often by parents, instead of attending school, it is called 'home education'.

Independent school - a school at which full-time education is provided for five or more children or young people of school age (whether or not such education is also provided for children or young people over that age), not being a public school or grant-aided school.

Individualised Educational Programme – a written document outlining the steps to be taken to help children and young people who have additional support needs to achieve specified learning outcomes.

Integrated Assessment Framework – a common means for all agencies and professionals to assess children's needs and to share information about them in order to ensure that interventions at any level lead to improvements in the child's life.

Local authority / council – local authorities and local councils are the same thing. They are run by local government and provide key services like education, social work and housing.

Looked-after children – a child or young person who is subject to an order such as a child protection order, a parental responsibilities order or a supervision requirement, either whilst living at home or being accommodated by the local authority.

Mainstream school – any school, primary or secondary, which caters for all children, not just those with specific needs. Education authorities run the vast majority of mainstream schools, though some are independent.

Mediation - a voluntary process whereby an independent third party seeks to help those in disagreement to reach an agreed resolution of their differences. It is most likely to be used when you and the education authority disagree about the support your child needs.

Medical assessment – would be carried out by a health professional (for example a doctor or nurse) and would look at health or medical issues that might affect your child's education.

Multiple needs – for the purposes of a co-ordinated support plan, these are factors which are not by themselves complex but when taken together, have or are likely to have a significant adverse effect on a child or young person's school education.

Parent – any person who is liable to maintain a child, has parental responsibilities or has care of a child or young person, including guardians.

Personal learning planning – the process by which children, young people and parents are involved in discussions with school about the goals of learning, including those for personal development. Its focus is on supporting dialogue and ultimately about engaging children and young people in their own learning.

Placing request – written request made to education authority for your child to attend a particular school.

Pre-school – in this handbook this means children who are aged three or four and who are using their free entitlement to pre-school education. In law this is called a 'prescribed pre-school child'.

Psychological assessment – an assessment carried out by a trained psychologist (for example an educational, occupational or clinical psychologist) to find out whether or not your child has learning difficulties, emotional or social difficulties or any other psychological condition.

Record of Needs – from the previous Special Educational Needs system, a Record of Needs was the formal plan of support to be provided to a child with SEN.

Respite services – short breaks away for people who need to be cared for, while making sure that their needs are still met. Respite may be for only a few hours or it may be for days at a time depending on the circumstances and support provided.

Review of co-ordinated support plan – if your child has a co-ordinated support plan it will be regularly reviewed to check that your child is receiving the right support.

School – a school means any primary, secondary or special school, and includes nursery schools and independent and grant-aided schools.

School age - generally from the age of 5 to 16 years.

School development plan – a plan which sets objectives for the school, schools have to prepare one every year.

Scottish Executive – the Scottish Executive is the devolved government of Scotland. The Scottish Executive is split into departments with responsibility for different areas, for example the Education Department.

Sheriff Court – a local court that deals with most civil litigation (including education law). The Sheriff is a legally qualified judge. There are Sheriff Courts in most towns and all cities.

Significant support – there is no legal definition of what significant support is but guidance says that it would be support that is at the higher end of what is available. It would be judged on the frequency, type and intensity of the support required. Significant support is one of the criteria for preparing a co-ordinated support plan.

Social work assessment – an assessment carried out by a social worker to look at particular issues in your child's life that may be affecting their ability to learn.

Special educational needs – a child had special educational needs if they had a learning difficulty which meant that they needed extra or specialised support. This term is no longer used. From November 2005 the wider term of additional support needs is used, which applies to anything that can result in additional needs, not just learning difficulties.

Special school – a school (or a special class or unit within a mainstream school) which provides education specially suited to the additional support needs of children or young people selected for attendance at the school, class or unit by reason of those needs.

Staged intervention – a system used by schools and nurseries to make sure that your child's difficulties are identified and supported as early as possible and with the least possible interruption and interference in their life.

Statement of Improvement Objectives – education authorities have to make an annual statement of improvement objectives to show how they are going to develop education services. School Development Plans are based on these objectives.

Supporter – someone you (or your child) chooses to be present and support you in any discussions with the school or education authority.

Transitions – changes in education, for example, starting nursery school, moving from primary to secondary school, transferring schools within or outwith an education authority's area.

Tribunals – Tribunals are not courts but they can make judgements about the law. Both the Additional Support Tribunal system and the Children's Hearing system are types of Tribunals.

Universal services – services which all children and young people have access to, for example health and education provision.

Unreasonable expenditure – a legal term which means that while the law says that the education authority must provide support, they do not have to do anything that involves spending an unreasonable amount. Unreasonable expenditure is to be judged on a case by case basis (see section 3.2 for more discussion).

Young carer – young person who provides care, usually to a family member.

Young person – under the Additional Support for Learning Act a young person is someone over school age (generally over 16 years) who is not yet 18 years of age.

7.2 Further information on some of the factors that might lead to additional support needs

The way in which circumstances affect your child will be unique to them. The question of whether a child has additional support needs or not can only be judged on an individual, case by case basis. It is not therefore possible to provide a definitive list of issues that may cause your child to have additional support needs. However this section aims to give you a bit more information about some common types of factors (many of which overlap with each other) that might result in a child or young person needing extra support with learning. It also gives some examples of the kinds of support that could be put in place for each one. In addition to the examples given here, your child's school/nursery must take more general action to improve access to education (see section 6.1 for information on accessibility strategies) and is expected make 'reasonable adjustments' to avoid discriminating against disabled children and young people (see section 6.1 for information on the Disability Discrimination Act).

Social circumstances

There are a vast range of circumstances which could cause problems with a child or young person's learning. If your child is experiencing a situation that is making it difficult for him/her to get the most out of education there is a range of support that could be put in place such as: counselling or other emotional support; involvement with a voluntary sector child or families project; extra help to catch up with missed school work; involvement of social work or mental health services; or flexibility with deadlines.

Some examples of social circumstances that might lead to a child or young person needing additional support at school are:

• family breakdown

• bereavement

• parental drug or alcohol abuse

• young person themselves becoming a parent

• caring responsibilities

• problems with offending behaviour

• child protection issues

• family member in prison

• parental physical or mental ill health

• housing issues such as poor housing or homelessness

• poverty.

Learning difficulties/learning disability

Having significantly more difficulty in learning compared with peers is one of the most common causes of additional support needs. Learning difficulties can vary enormously and range from difficulties in acquiring basic intellectual, physical or social skills (affecting a very small percentage of children and young people), to specific problems with particular tasks like number and reading work (affecting a large number of children and young people). Some learning difficulties can be identified at birth, such as Down's Syndrome, while others can take longer to come to light or can be acquired as a result of an accident or illness. Some children and young people have learning difficulties which do not appear to have any physical cause and might have been caused by a lack of proper stimulation or learning opportunities. Some children with physical disabilities or emotional problems might also have learning difficulties.

Learning difficulties may relate to one or more of the following areas of a child or young person's life:

- functioning physically, learning through practice or experience, responding to surroundings
- understanding the meanings of words, or symbols, memorising, grasping ideas, reasoning, making connections, problem solving, and so on
- recognising shapes, sizes, pictures or configurations, sound patterns, etc; relating objects to one another, judging distances and so on
- communicating with others, developing orderly behaviour, carrying out routine everyday tasks.

These difficulties may vary from very mild to severe, some may be overcome with the right sort of help while others may be lifelong and require continuing support (most probably lie somewhere between these extremes). Most of these difficulties are likely to affect how children learn to build up vocabulary, read and write, handle and measure quantities and shapes, draw comparisons and connections, conduct experiments, and more generally do things and find out things for themselves.

The kind of additional support your child might receive if he/she has a learning difficulty includes:

- additional help in pre-school to prepare for starting formal education
- an adapted curriculum tailored to your child's particular learning needs (for example with greater attention on reading or number work) and designed to allow his/her abilities to develop

- extra tuition designed around your child's individual needs
- creating school surroundings which are comfortable and stimulating for your child, for example making sure the school and classroom is laid out so that it is easy for your child to find their way around
- maximising the opportunities your child is given, for example through training in everyday skills and tasks; work experience placements; extra-curricular activities; and flexibility in the school timetable
- school staff varying their teaching methods to respond to your child's needs.

Social, emotional and behavioural difficulties

Children and young people can have social, emotional and behavioural difficulties (often referred to as SEBD) for many different reasons. These difficulties can be temporary or ongoing and can vary from mild to severe. More serious social, emotional and behavioural difficulties can result in a child being excluded from school but the school should do everything it can to support the child and prevent this from happening. If your child is excluded, this should only be a short term solution and the education authority must make sure your child continues to receive full-time education (see section 6.3 for more on exclusions).

The term 'social, emotional and behavioural difficulties' encompasses a wide range of behavioural issues which might cause problems such as inability to concentrate on learning; poor attendance at school; lack of challenge in the curriculum; difficulties joining in and getting along with classmates and school staff; lack of understanding of consequences; and difficulty obeying boundaries and following school rules.

The kind of additional support your child might receive if he/she has social, emotional and behavioural difficulties includes:

- extra attention from a classroom assistant or learning support auxiliary

- systems to help with behaviour management, for example a 'time out' space that your child can go to if they are feeling angry or upset
- support from a social worker or specialist in child psychology and behaviour
- placement in a school specifically for children and young people with behavioural difficulties (this would only be likely if your child's social, emotional and behavioural difficulties were severe, see section 6.4 on mainstreaming for more information).

Hearing difficulties

Hearing loss or difficulty can have various causes and can range in severity including:

- children and young people who cannot hear at all and who may have related speech and language difficulties
- children and young people who have partial hearing, who cannot hear sounds properly in terms of loudness, pitch or range (some children have difficulties in hearing or distinguishing between certain word or letter sounds), and
- children who can hear properly but have difficulty in listening to or concentrating on what is said, for example because of language barriers, poor concentration, emotional issues, or other factors.

These difficulties may affect a child or young person's speech, pronunciation or use of language and may also have an effect on their learning or on social and personality development. However hearing difficulties will not lead to additional support needs in all children and young people. This will depend on the individual child or young person and their learning environment.

The kind of additional support your child might receive if he/she has social, hearing difficulties includes:

- a loop system in the classroom
- awareness on the part of school staff, for example always facing your child if he/she lip-reads

- speech and language therapy
- teaching sign language to classmates and school staff
- visits from a teacher of the deaf
- non-audio fire alarm
- support from a specialist voluntary organisation.

Visual difficulties

These range from complete or partial loss of sight to other problems such as difficulty in focusing, hand-eye co-ordination, and perception. These can begin at birth or can happen later in a child's life, for example through injury or illness. Visual difficulties could make it hard for your child to cope with the school or nursery environment and might affect particular areas of their learning such as reading, writing and participating in practical lessons.

Some specific types of visual difficulties include:

- very poor eyesight, blurred or distorted vision, inability to read print at all, though possibly with an ability to distinguish between shapes or colours
- problems in focusing due to long or short sight; double vision; limited range of vision; colour blindness; night blindness
- poor hand-eye co-ordination resulting in difficulties with tasks such as copying or operating equipment
- difficulties recognising (and often copying) patterns, shapes, letters or words (this type of visual difficulty can be associated with conditions like dyslexia).

The kind of additional support your child might receive if he/she has visual difficulties includes:

- adaptations to the curriculum to enable your child to take part in the full range of lessons and activities
- information in alternative formats such as audio CD or tape, Braille or large print
- visual aids such as hand-held or standing magnifiers

- special or extra lighting, best positioning of your child's desk (for example to minimise glare or shadow), or special furniture, such as a sloping desk top
- assistance from a learning auxiliary.

Mobility difficulties

There are a range of mobility difficulties, some of which are related to disability or health issues. Some children and young people will have mobility difficulties from birth whilst others might acquire these later as a result of an illness, accident or progressive condition. Children and young people who develop mobility difficulties, and their parents, often find this difficult to come to terms with and adjust to. Some of the types of additional support your child might receive if he/she has mobility difficulties include:

- physical adaptations to the school/nursery (for example modification of equipment, toilets, entrances/exits, desks and seating), possibly including provision of ramps, handrails/holds and lifts
- physiotherapy and/or occupational therapy
- specialist equipment, for example to aid reading or writing
- mobility aids such as artificial limbs or wheelchairs
- specialist counselling and social support for children and young people who need help coming to terms with a mobility difficulty.

Speech or language difficulties

A large number of children and young people will have speech or language difficulties at some point. These difficulties can be caused by physiological, social, emotional or cultural factors and include issues such as:

- no verbal communication
- difficulties with making word sounds, for example as a result of a condition such as cerebral palsy or cleft palate
- difficulties in putting words together, perhaps because of a learning or emotional difficulty

- difficulties with understanding or expression of language
- hesitant or confused speech including stuttering or stammering, possibly caused by nervousness or other emotional issues.

The kind of additional support your child might receive if he/she has speech or language difficulties includes:

- extra language tuition at the appropriate rate for your child
- specialised approach from your child's classroom teacher (often this will be done in close partnership with you; many speech and language difficulties can be solved easily by using a specialised approach integrated into day to day learning both at school and home)
- speech and language therapy
- use of alternative communication formats (for example sign language or symbol systems which are often used with children and young people with little or no verbal communication)
- communication aids such as an electronic speaker.

Health issues

Certain illnesses or medical conditions may result in a child or young person needing additional support with learning, for example some health issues are likely to mean that a child or young person is absent from school frequently and/or for prolonged periods of time.

The kind of additional support your child might receive if he/she has health issues includes:

- special arrangements for medication to be given at school (see section 6.4)
- adapting or relaxing the demands normally made on pupils, for example by giving your child more time to complete work or making allowances if necessary in particular areas such as physical education
- home or hospital schooling by specialist education authority staff (your child has a right to education and they should continue to receive education as far as possible while they are ill)

- protecting your child (without being overprotective) from things which may aggravate health problems, for example irritants such as school pets, extremes of temperature, air impurities, or flashing lights

- provision of appropriate food, for example extra snacks available for your child if he/she is diabetic

- alternative arrangements for exams, such as being able to sit them in hospital.

7.3 Information on specific conditions

You can get more detailed information on specific conditions from many of the voluntary organisations listed at the back of this handbook. One very commonly used resource is the publication produced by Contact a Family called The Contact a Family Directory of Specific Conditions and Rare Disorders. The following information gives you a short overview of a number of the common conditions which lead to children and young people needing extra support with learning.

Autistic spectrum disorders

These include a number of related conditions including autism and Asperger Syndrome. Autism is an ongoing developmental disability that affects how a child or young person relates to their environment (including people). Autism can result in a child having problems relating to others and understanding emotions and expressions. Children and young people with autism often have speech and language difficulties and may find multi-sensory environments and changes to familiar routines extremely upsetting. Asperger Syndrome is similar to autism but has far milder symptoms and does not generally lead to learning or speech and language difficulties (although it may still mean that your child needs additional support at school/nursery).

Brain injury

An acquired brain injury (ABI) is an injury to the brain that has happened since birth. It could be the result of an accident, illness such as an infection, stroke, tumour or poisoning. The injury can affect the way a person thinks, feels and behaves and can, but not always, affect them physically. The majority of children who sustain mild brain injury require no surgery but can experience learning difficulties, emotional and behavioural problems which can sometimes take years to become apparent. Brain injury is a life-long condition; it is known as 'the hidden disability' and 1 in 25 children in Scotland attend A&E as a result of a head injury every year.

Cerebral palsy

This is a term which covers a number of non-progressive (though not necessarily unchanging) motor impairment conditions which range from having a severe impact to having almost none. Cerebral palsy is thought to happen due to damage to the brain before, or during, birth and is often detected at an early age. Some of the possible effects of cerebral palsy include movement difficulties, hearing or visual impairment, learning difficulties (this includes problems with speech and language), and related health issues. Cerebral palsy ranges vastly in the way it affects children and young people.

Chronic Fatigue Syndrome (ME/Post Viral Syndrome)

Chronic Fatigue Syndrome is a viral infection (often known as Post Viral Syndrome or ME) associated with symptoms such as fatigue, anxiety, depression, gastric problems, loss of concentration or memory, and disturbed sleep. There is not widely effective treatment but there are a number of ways in which people with Chronic Fatigue Syndrome manage their symptoms (for more information on this contact one of the specialist organisations in section 7.6 of this handbook) and most recover completely.

Cystic fibrosis

This an inherited disorder affecting the lungs and digesting system and causing breathing difficulties, coughing, lung infections, malnourishment, and restricted growth. It is the most commonly inherited disorder among children in the UK and it can be life threatening. Cystic fibrosis does not normally cause learning difficulties but can lead to prolonged and/or frequent absences from school. Children and young people with cystic fibrosis may also need special diets and supplements, medication, frequent toileting, physiotherapy and breathing exercise while at school. They may also have to avoid physical activities or exertion in hot weather (which can result in exhaustion due to excessive loss of salt through perspiration).

Deaf-blindness

Children and young people who are both deaf and blind suffer some of the worst difficulties affecting learning and personal development. This condition usually begins at birth, mainly as a result of the mother catching German measles (Rubella) in the first three months of pregnancy. Some children have partial sight and/or hearing at birth, which can be prolonged with treatment, although there may be some deterioration later on. Children and young people who are deaf-blind may also have heart or brain damage and difficulties with hyperactivity. Although learning may be slow deaf-blind children and young people can, and do, make progress.

Epilepsy

Epilepsy is a neurological disorder which affects around 1 in 200 people. It can begin before birth or develop at any stage of life (including as a result of an accident or illness). Epilepsy affects different people in different ways but always involves having repeated seizures. There are different types of seizures but one which can affect children is 'absence seizures' where a child has brief moments of lost consciousness (often many times a day) where they stop suddenly and stare blankly. Epilepsy does not necessarily lead to learning difficulties but is common among children with severe learning difficulties. Some types of epilepsy can also affect verbal or practical skills and can be related to behaviour problems.

Friedreich's ataxia

This is a disorder of the nervous system which causes a weakening of the leg, arm, hand, eye and ear muscles (but not affecting brain function in any way). Although children and young people with Friedreich's ataxia do not have learning difficulties, they do tend to have frequent absences from school and may be affected by mobility, speech, hearing and visual difficulties.

Multiple injuries

These can result from accidents or injuries at birth or during childhood, for example a car accident. Children and young people with multiple injuries may have to spend long periods away from school, either in hospital or at home, and may require regular nursing or medical attention at school or nursery. Depending on the nature of their injuries a child or young person might have difficulties in mobility, speech, hearing, sight, learning and so on. These difficulties may be temporary or permanent and a child or young person might need support to come to terms with the emotional impact of an injury.

Spina bifida and hydrocephalus

Spina bifida is caused by the bones of the spine not closing properly and so leaving the nerves of the spinal chord exposed. Spina bifida happens early on in pregnancy and can be operated on soon after birth. The extent to which spina bifida affects a child or young person varies but can include loss of sensation in parts of the body below the spine to complete paralysis. It is often accompanied by hydrocephalus which is a build-up of fluid around the brain. Children and young people with spina bifida and hydrocephalus may need physiotherapy and can suffer from incontinence, epilepsy, poor hand-eye co-ordination, perceptual difficulties, learning difficulties and concentration problems.

7.4 Professionals who work in the additional support needs field

If your child has additional support needs, there are a wide variety of professionals who may help to support them. This section outlines the jobs of some of the most common staff that you and your child may come into contact with.

Class Teacher – teachers have been specially trained and are registered with the General Teaching Council for Scotland. Class teachers are likely to have most day to day contact with your child and will be involved in assessing whether or not your child has additional needs and providing support to them. In primary school, most children will only have one class teacher, however in secondary school where time is divided into subjects, there will be a number of different teachers working with your child.

Clinical Psychologist – a trained psychologist who specialises in behavioural and emotional issues. Clinical psychologists can help parents and children to identify strengths and needs, and to incorporate appropriate goals into individual programme plans. Clinical psychologists can help alleviate difficulties in social skills, communication, developmental delay, anxiety and sensory impairments, and will be able to deal with issues around resettlement from hospital and the development of community services. They offer support to carers, including families.

Director of Education – sometimes called Director of Children's Services, each education authority has a Director who has overall responsibility for all the services provided by the authority. The Director will deal with situations that have not been resolved at school level or by the education authority officers, particularly in relation to the resources available to support your child. Your local council switchboard can tell you the name of the Director of Education for your area.

Education Authority Officer – usually based in the education authority rather than the school, officers provide advice and support to parents and in some cases children and young people. They can help to resolve disagreements with the school and can help you to access services and support. Often it will be the education authority officer who decides what amount of support can be provided to your child, on the basis of the assessments carried out.

Educational Psychologist – a trained psychologist who specialises in how children learn and develop. They will have a teaching qualification and a post-graduate qualification to become an educational psychologist. Educational psychologists use tests to help identify what additional support your child might need, taking into account things like their communication skills, personal and social skills, approach and attitude to learning, educational attainment, self-image, interests and behaviour. In some cases, educational psychologists will offer support and counselling to children and their families. Often the educational psychologist will work for the education authority, but if you disagree with the conclusions or support provided by the education authority you may want to commission an independent educational psychologist to carry out an assessment on your behalf. The British Psychological Society has a directory of Chartered Psychologists that you can use to find one in your area (see section 7.6 for contacts).

Education Welfare Officer - also known as education social workers, deal with young people who have problems with irregular attendance or absence from school. They investigate the reasons behind the absence, which may include problems relating to health, family, bullying or working illegally. Education welfare officers work with social work departments to support children involved in child protection procedures.

English as an Additional Language Teacher / Assistant – someone with expertise in teaching children and young people for whom English is not their first language.

Guidance Teacher – many education authority secondary schools in Scotland have guidance teachers. The job of a guidance teacher is to:

• help pupils with personal problems such as bullying or behavioural difficulties (personal guidance)

• help pupils make informed subject choices at transitions from S2 to S3, S4 to S5 and S5 to S6, and to monitor their progress and attainments across all subjects (curricular guidance)

• assist pupils in making choices about careers and further or higher education (vocational guidance).

Guidance teachers are often responsible for preparing and teaching programmes of personal and social education, which deal with matters of health, relationships and careers, among other things. They usually have about 100-150 pupils in their care.

Head Teacher – your child's head teacher has responsibility for running the school, including the additional support being planned or provided for your child. The Head Teacher is likely to attend meetings and work with you to make sure that your child's needs are met. As the schools manager, the head teacher can allocate resources to your child if they need additional support. In some cases, if the school is large, the head teacher may have delegated this to another suitably qualified teacher. If you have any complaints about the way your child's additional support is being provided, or if you are unhappy with anything in the school, you should talk to the head teacher about it and they should try to resolve it for you.

Health Visitor – health visitors, sometimes called public health nurses, are nurses who visit parents with children under five years old at home and advise them on areas such as hygiene, safety, feeding, sleeping, teething, immunisation and managing difficult behaviour. Health visitors work for the National Health Service (NHS) and are qualified registered nurses or midwives.

Learning Support Teacher – learning support teachers are qualified teachers who specialise in working with children with additional support needs. They have a varied role: they may train and support class/subject teachers to make sure that the curriculum is accessible, or work directly with children and young people either individually or in groups. The learning support teacher may co-ordinate the support provided to your child and may be your key contact at the school. Not all schools have learning support teachers.

Nursery Manager - the manager of a pre-school establishment, which could be run by the education authority or by a private or voluntary organisation.

Nursery Nurse / Assistant – also known as early education and childcare workers. Nursery nurses work in early years and pre-school settings providing care and education to 0 – 5 year olds. There are recognised qualifications in early years care and education and more and more nursery nurses are qualified.

Occupational Therapist – occupational therapists are qualified health care professionals who assess and treat physical and psychiatric conditions to help people do the things that they want to. Occupational therapists work in hospital and other settings, including schools. An occupational therapist can help people learn new ways of doing things, adapt materials or equipment, or make changes to where people live and work to make them accessible.

Paediatrician – a qualified doctor who specialises in child health. Your child may be referred to a paediatrician by your GP or someone else who is working with you and your child. They may carry out medical assessments, prescribe medication or treatments or offer support and advice.

Peripatetic Teacher – teachers who visit different schools, rather than being based in one, are known as peripatetic. They tend to be highly specialised, for example in sensory disabilities or speech and language.

Physiotherapist – healthcare professionals that help and treat people with physical problems caused by illness or accident. In child health, they often work with children who have learning disabilities or severe mental and physical disabilities. Physiotherapists help people to get as much physical movement as they can by health promotion, preventive healthcare, treatment and rehabilitation.

Psychiatrist – a medical doctor who specialises in emotional and behavioural problems. Your GP or other health professional will refer your child to a psychiatrist if they think it would help. Some psychiatrists specialise in children and teenagers. A psychiatrist will talk to you and your child and look at your medical history and the medical history of other members of the family. A psychiatric examination may involve talking, drawing, or playing with toys to help the psychiatrist better understand what is going on. Questions may be asked about the child or adolescent's view of the problem, as well as how the child is getting along with family, friends, teachers, and students in school. An assessment is made of the child or adolescent's strengths as well as their problems. Child and Adolescent Psychiatrists use a variety of treatment techniques, for example psychotherapies, behaviour therapies, medication or working with the school and family.

School Nurse – a qualified registered nurse may be employed by the Health Board to work with pupils, teachers and parents to promote the health of children at school. The School Nurse may provide health education and be involved in immunisation programmes. They may help to support children with additional needs, for example by helping them take their medicine, talking to them about their situation or working with the other school staff to make sure that they understand your child's needs. If you are worried about your child, the School Nurse may be able to offer you advice and support as well.

Speech and Language Therapist – a specialist in communication disorders. Speech and language therapists work to assess, diagnose and develop a programme of care to maximize the communication potential of the people under their care/referred to them. Speech and language therapists also work to support people with swallowing, eating and drinking difficulties. They work with children who have a range of additional support needs, including:

• mild, moderate or severe learning difficulties

• physical disability

• language delay arising from any source, including deprivation

• specific language impairment

• specific difficulties in producing sounds

• hearing impairment

• cleft palate

• stammering/dysfluency

- autism/social interaction difficulties
- dyslexia.

Social Worker – works with people, often at times of difficulty, to help them solve problems and improve their well-being. Social workers are based in the local authority social work department (or equivalent) and work closely with colleagues in health and education to support children and families. The type of support provided depends on your family's needs but social workers are able to arrange respite services, parenting classes, benefits and debt advice, advocacy services, befriending, childcare. Social workers have professional qualifications and are registered by the Scottish Social Services Council.

Teaching/classroom Assistant – also known as learning support assistants or special needs assistants or auxiliaries. Teaching/classroom assistants work under the direction of the teacher. Many teaching/classroom assistants are employed with specific responsibilities to work with individual pupils; others are given more general classroom responsibilities. Both roles are key to supporting inclusion by facilitating participation and learning, helping to build confidence, self-esteem and independence so that all pupils are enabled to reach their full potential alongside their peers. Assistants may have had some training but they will not have formal teaching qualifications.

Teacher of the deaf – a teacher who is also specifically qualified to teach deaf children and who will often provide support to deaf children as well as to their parents and other professionals (for example other teachers).

7.5 Reading list

The reading list below has been drawn up to provide sources of information on:

- other guides to additional support for learning
- your child's needs
- teaching and learning resources.

The list does not include all the publications that you might find helpful but we have tried to include a cross-section of books and leaflets, many of which will signpost you to other sources of information. Most of the publications listed here should be available through your local library – even if the library does not have them in stock they should be able to arrange for a copy through an inter-library loan. Some of the books and leaflets are published by voluntary organisations who may be able to send you free copies either by post or on the internet. The information provided will tell you if this is the case. Alternatively you may be able to buy them in bookshops or online through the publisher's website.

Some of the books listed are written in relation to England and Wales so the legal information will not apply in Scotland. However they have been listed because of the general information and guidance that they contain. Some of the publications also refer to the old Special Educational Needs system which operated until November 2005. Again, the general information on your child's needs will still be relevant but some of the information on the law will now be out of date.

Other guides to Additional Support for Learning

Enquire (2005) Parents' Guide to Additional Support for Learning, Edinburgh: Children in Scotland

> Enquire and the Scottish Executive have produced this free, comprehensive and up-to-date guide to the education system and children with additional support needs, listing the rights of parents, useful organisations and how to become more involved in a child's education. This guide is available in the following formats: English, Braille, large print, audio cassette, Hindi, Punjabi, Urdu, Gaelic, Chinese and Arabic. Contact Enquire for a copy (see section 7.6 for contact details).

Enquire (2005) guides for children and young people

> See section 7.7 Resources for your child for further information

Scottish Executive (2005) Supporting Children's Learning: The Code of Practice

The Scottish Executive guidance on the implementation of the Additional Support for Learning Act. This publication is free and you can get a copy from Blackwell's Bookshop (0131 622 8283) or online at www.ltscotland.org.uk.

Skill Scotland (2005) Opportunities at 16 Edinburgh: Skill Scotland

A free guide for young people on their choices at 16. You can get a copy from Skill Scotland (see section 7.6 for contact details).

The policy and legislative background

Additional Support for Learning Act Implementation Newsletters

The newsletters contain important up-to-date information about the Additional Support for Learning Act, its implementation and where more detailed information can be accessed.

Available at: www.enquire.org.uk

Scottish Executive (2003) Report of the consultation on the draft Additional Support for Learning Bill Edinburgh: Scottish Executive

Scottish Executive (2003) Moving Forward! Additional support for learning Edinburgh: Scottish Executive

Scottish Executive (2002) Assessing our children's educational needs: The Way Forward? Scottish Executive response to the consultation Edinburgh: Scottish Executive

Scottish Parliament Education, Culture and Sport Committee (2001) Report on the Inquiry into Special Educational Needs Edinburgh: Scottish Parliament

Scottish Executive (1999) Improving our schools: special educational needs: the Scottish Executive response to the Report of the Advisory Committee on the Education of Children with Severe Low Incidence Disabilities Edinburgh: Scottish Executive

Scottish Executive (1999) Advisory Committee Report into the Education of Children with Severe Low Incidence Disabilities. Edinburgh: Scottish Executive

Scottish Executive (1999) Implementing Inclusiveness, Realising Potential - The Beattie Committee Report Edinburgh: Scottish Executive

Scottish Office (1998) Special educational needs in Scotland: a discussion paper Edinburgh: Scottish Office (now Scottish Executive)

Your child's needs

Finding out that your child has a specific condition, or is going through a difficult time, can be a traumatic experience and often you will want to find out as much information as possible. Here we have listed some of the organisations that can help provide you with detailed information about a range of conditions or situations. There are more organisations listed in section 7.6 of this handbook.

Most of the information listed below is available free, either on the internet or by contacting the relevant organisation (see section 7.6 for full contact details including web addresses).

Afasic

Afasic is a UK charity representing children and young adults with communication impairments. It produces information sheets explaining terms used in relation to children with speech and language impairments. While these are aimed at professionals, parents may find these sheets useful and informative. They have information sheets on:

- Specific language impairment
- Dyslexia/specific learning difficulties
- Developmental language delay/disorder
- Learning difficulties
- Semantic and pragmatic disorders
- Selective mutism
- Autism
- The autistic spectrum
- Alternative/augmentative communication

- Articulation
- Asperger's syndrome
- Stammering
- Higher level language disorder
- Phonological problems
- Expressive language difficulties
- Pervasive developmental disorders
- Aphasia/dysphasia
- Dyspraxia
- Fragile X syndrome
- Downs syndrome
- Dysarthria
- Comprehension or receptive language difficulties
- Landau Kleffner syndrome
- Epilepsy
- Auditory sequential memory
- Specific Memory Disorders: Short term memory
- Specific Memory Disorders: Long term memory

ChildLine Scotland

ChildLine Scotland produces a wide range of publications on key issues affecting children and young people. These publications are aimed at children and young people, parents and carers, childcare professionals, teachers, and the general public and include the following topics:

- Alcohol
- Bereavement (when someone dies)
- Bullying
- Child abuse
- Children in care
- Domestic violence
- Eating problems
- Exam stress
- HIV and AIDS
- Homelessness and runaways
- Pregnancy and contraception
- Racism

- The rights of children and young people
- Self-harm
- Stepfamilies
- Suicide

Contact a Family

Contact a Family maintains a database with information about a substantial number of specific conditions and rare disorders which you can access from its website. Each entry contains a short medical description of the condition together with details of inheritance patterns and prenatal diagnosis. This information is followed by details of the related support networks, their activities, publication, and what they offer to families.

Mental Health Foundation

The Mental Health Foundation produces factsheets on:

- Alcoholism and Alcohol Abuse
- Anorexia Nervosa
- Anti Social Personality Disorder
- Anxiety
- Anxious Personality Disorder
- Attention Deficit Hyperactivity Disorder (ADHD)
- Bulimia Nervosa
- Dementia
- Dependant Personality Disorder
- Depression
- Eating Disorders
- Emotionally Unstable Personality Disorder
- Hearing voices
- Histrionic Personality Disorder
- Hyperactivity
- Insomnia
- Mania
- Manic Depression
- Narcissistic Personality Disorder
- Narcolepsy
- Neurosis
- Obsessive-compulsive disorder (OCD)
- Obsessive Compulsive Personality Disorder
- Panic Attacks
- Paranoia
- Paranoid Personality

Disorder

- Personality Disorders

- Phobias

- Post Natal Depression (Postpartum Illness)

- Post traumatic stress disorder

- Psychosis

- Schizoaffective Disorder

- Schizoid Personality Disorder

- Schizophrenia

- Schizotypal Personality Disorder

- Seasonal Affective Disorder (SAD)

- Self harm

- Sleep Disorders

- Stress

- Substance Abuse

- Suicide

Parentline Scotland

Produce a number of general factsheets about issues of interest to parents, including:

- Worried about a child?

- Relationships between parents and teenagers

- Factsheet for Dads

- Family relationships

- Bullying

Teaching and learning resources

Abbott, Chris (2002) Special educational needs and the internet: issues for the inclusive classroom London: Routledge/Falmer

> With internet access for every school now a reality, teachers are beginning to explore the use of the internet in the education of children with special needs. This book describes its benefits for children across the spectrum of special educational needs, from those with physical disabilities or sensory impairment to those with learning or social difficulties. With contributions from leading practitioners in the field, this book addresses the huge range of possibilities the internet and associated technology offer for these pupils.

Afasic Communication in the classroom Kent: Afasic

A handbook for parents, teachers and therapists working with children and young people with communication difficulties in the classroom. From Afasic South Kent, Stoneleigh, Church Road, Mersham, near Ashford, Kent TN25 6NT

Closs, Alison (ed.) (2000) The education of children with medical conditions London: D. Fulton Publishers

This book examines the issues which affect the participation, achievement and social inclusion of children with medical conditions in education. The contributors discuss areas of potential difficulty and suggest ways of developing more effective and efficient provision, in and out of school. This approach includes young people's, parents' and siblings' accounts, professional descriptions and critiques of research, educational policies and practices within the UK.

Cunningham, Sally and MacFarlane, Brenda (2004) Additional support needs: Advice on the implementation of supported units at Access 1 Dundee: Learning and Teaching Scotland

This guide has been produced to support the implementation of six 'Healthy Basic Cooking' units. Descriptions of levels of support, language and communication approaches, multi-sensory approaches, progression and assessment advice are provided. Examples of different models of support are provided.

HMIe How good is our school?: Inclusion and Equality (2003) Edinburgh: HMIe

Series of three guides that provide self-evaluation tools for schools and local authorities. 'Evaluating education and care placements for looked after children and young people', 'Evaluating education for pupils with additional support needs in mainstream schools' and 'Promoting Race Equality'. Parents may find the quality and standards information provided of interest.

Learning and Teaching Scotland Support for Learning: Special Educational Needs within the 5-14 Curriculum Dundee: Learning and Teaching Scotland

> The 5-14 programme provides a common curricular framework that, if properly used, ensures appropriate education for all pupils and removes barriers in the way of professional collaboration between teachers and members of support services in mainstream and special schools and units. The Support for Learning series contains information and suggestions for staff development activities in the appraisal and planning processes.

Macintyre, Christine (2002) Play for children with special needs: including children aged 3 – 8 London: David Fulton

> This book aims to help practitioners to ensure that they are doing all they can to include children with special educational needs. The author looks at several conditions such as Asperger's Syndrome, dyslexia, dyspraxia, Down's Syndrome and ADD/ADHD and shows how play can be adapted to help alleviate the difficulties children with these additional needs might have.

Scottish Executive (2003) Inclusive schooling: Enhancing policy and practice Edinburgh: Scottish Executive

> An interactive professional development resource that supports educational establishments and councils in the ongoing development of consistent and coherent policies for inclusive practice.

Scottish Executive, LT Scotland, CERES, City of Edinburgh Council (2003) Educating for race equality: a toolkit for Scottish teachers Edinburgh: Scottish Executive

> A CD-ROM and web resource designed to support teachers as they become more knowledgeable about education for race equality and anti-racism within the curriculum and wider life of schools.

Smyth, Geri (2003) Helping bilingual pupils to access the curriculum London: David Fulton

This book offers practical guidance for teachers working with bilingual pupils in mainstream primary and secondary education and aims to help teachers make the curriculum as accessible as possible to these children. It provides examples of the good practice that has evolved around teaching bilingual children in the classroom.

Wolfendale, Sheila (2003) Special educational needs in the early years: snapshots of practice London: Routledge/Falmer

This book is a practical and accessible guide to teaching young children with special educational needs. At the heart of the book is the belief that the focus should be on the child as an active learner, rather than on their disability. The author addresses key issues such as the nature and causes of specific disabilities, intervention and assessment, working with families, planning individualised objectives and instructional strategies. There are also new sections on emotional competence, early literacy concerns and discussions of the emotional implications of brain research. Case study examples and practical suggestions are included throughout.

Other useful books

Beveridge, Sally (1999) Special educational needs in schools London: Routledge

Effective communication between the home and school is crucial for any child's education, but where special needs are concerned, creating good partnerships is essential. This book debates issues such as the importance of community, interactions between the child and their family, and how to promote parental involvement.

Booth, Tony and Ainscow, Mel (eds.) (1998) From them to us: an international study of inclusion in education London: Routledge

Inclusive education has become a phrase with international currency shaping the content of conferences and national educational policies around the world. But what does it mean? Is it about including a special group of disabled learners or students seen to have 'special needs' (them) or is it concerned with making educational institutions inclusive, responsive to the diversity of all their students (us)? In this unique comparative study, the editors have brought together an international team of researchers from eight countries to develop case studies which explore the processes of inclusion and exclusion within a school or group of schools set in its local and national context.

Clark, Catherine, Dyson, Alan and Millward, Alan (eds) (1998) Theorising special education London: Routledge

The field of special needs education is well established, and although it continues to develop in exciting and controversial ways, involving some of education's leading thinkers, many people feel it is lacking a coherent theoretical analysis of its own. This book brings together contributions from key names in the field from the UK and beyond.

Cole, Mike (ed.) (2000) Education, equality and human rights: Issues of gender, 'race', sexuality, special needs and social class London: Falmer

A comprehensive study and reference book on equality and education. It addresses the issues of human rights and their relationship to education. Race, disability, gender, sexuality and social class are all covered.

Riddell, Sheila (2002) Special educational needs Edinburgh: Dunedin Academic Press

Discusses the nature of school inclusion, its relationship with social inclusion more widely and the compatibility of the raising standards and social inclusion agendas. The provisions and implications of new legislation prohibiting discrimination against disabled children in schools are discussed.

Scottish Consumer Council (2004) A – Z Scots Education Law Edinburgh: TSO

Provides parents, children and others with a handy reference to education law in Scotland. It covers the whole spectrum of the law to do with education including choice of school, the curriculum, discipline, human rights, homework, safety and supervision, school closures and transport and many, many more.

7.6 Contacts and websites

ADDISS (Attention Deficit Disorder Information and Support Service)

Website: www.addiss.co.uk

Description: ADDISS provides information, training and support for parents, sufferers and professionals in the fields of ADHD and related learning and behavioural difficulties. All our activity is supported by our Professional Board of expert advisers.

Contact: 10 Station Road
             Mill Hill
             London
             NW7 2JU

             Tel: 020 8906 9068
             Fax: 020 8959 0727
             Email: info@addiss.co.uk

Barnardo's Scotland

Website: www.barnardos.org.uk

Description: Barnardo's Scotland works to help vulnerable children and young people transform their lives and fulfil their potential. It runs projects providing education support and dealing with a vast range of issues including: disability, poverty, abuse, HIV/AIDS, family breakdown, youth crime, homelessness, alcohol or drug misuse, and looked-after children.

Contact: Barnardo's Scotland
             Headquarters
             235 Corstorphine Road
             Edinburgh
             EH12 7AR

             Tel: 0131 316 4008

Capability Scotland

Website: www.capability-scotland.org.uk

Description: Capability Scotland is Scotland's leading disability organisation. We provide a range of flexible services which support disabled people of all ages in their everyday lives. We are committed to creating a just and fair Scotland and we work with disabled people, their families and carers to influence policy legislation, practice and attitudes.

Contact: Advice Service
Capability Scotland
11 Ellersly Road
Edinburgh
EH12 6HY

Tel: 0131 313 5510
Textphone: 0131 346 2529
Email: ascs@capability-scotland.org.uk

Careers Scotland

Website: www.careers-scotland.org.uk

Description: We provide services, information and support to individuals at all ages and stages of career planning and employers wanting to recruit and maintain a productive workforce.

Contact: Careers Scotland Headquarters
150 Broomielaw
Atlantic Quay
Glasgow
G2 8LU

Tel No: 08458 502 502

Child Brain Injury Trust

Website: www.cbituk.org

Description: The Child Brain Injury (CBIT) supports anyone in the United Kingdom affected by childhood acquired brain injury. We provide information, support and training to families and professionals.

An acquired brain injury is sometimes referred to as hidden disability, and often goes unrecognised. This inevitably leads to problems for a child in terms of education, provision of care and support.

Contact: Princes House
5 Shandwick Place
Edinburgh
EH2 4RG

Tel: 0131 229 1852
Email: jennyhill@cbituk.org

ChildLine Scotland

Website: www.childline.org.uk/Scotland.asp

Description: ChildLine Scotland is the free telephone helpline for any child or young person with any problem.

Contact: ChildLine Scotland
18 Albion Street
Glasgow
G1 1LH

Tel: 0870 336 2910
Fax: 0870 336 2911
Helpline number: 0800 1111

Children in Scotland

Website: www.childreninscotland.org.uk

Description: Children in Scotland is a national agency for voluntary, statutory and professional organisations and individuals working with children and their families in Scotland. It provides advocacy and mediation in relation to the Education (Additional Support for Learning) (Scotland) Act.

Contact: Princes House
5 Shandwick Place
Edinburgh
EH2 4RG

Tel: 0131 228 8484
Fax: 0131 228 8585
Email: info@childreninscotland.org.uk

Citizens Advice Scotland

Website: www.cas.org.uk

Description: The Scottish CAB service is united by two aims: to ensure that individuals do not suffer through lack of knowledge of their rights and responsibilities, or of the services available to them, or through an inability to express their need effectively and, equally to exercise a responsible influence on the development of social policies and services, both locally and nationally. CAS and Scottish bureaux work together to achieve these aims.

Contact: Spectrum House
2 Powderhall Road
Edinburgh
EH7 4GB

Tel. 0131 550 1000
Fax. 0131 550 1001

Commission for Racial Equality

Website: www.cre.gov.uk/scotland

Description: CRE Scotland work for a just and integrated Scotland, where diversity is valued. We use both persuasion and our powers under the law to give everyone an equal chance to live free from fear, discrimination, prejudice and racism.

Contact: The Tun
12 Jackson's Entry
off Holyrood Road
Edinburgh
EH8 8PJ

Tel: 0131 524 2000
Fax: 0131 524 2001
Textphone: 0131 524 2018
Email: scotland@cre.gov.uk

Contact a Family Scotland

Website: www.cafamily.org.uk

Description: Contact a family is a UK-wide charity providing support, advice and information for families who care for children with any disability or additional need.

Contact: Norton Park
57 Albion Street
Edinburgh
EH7 5QY

Tel: 0131 475 2608
Fax: 0131 475 2609
Textphone: 0808 808 3556
Freephone (10am-4pm, Mon-Fri) 0808 808 3555
Email: scotland@cafamily.org.uk

Cruse Bereavement Care Scotland

Website: www.crusescotland.org.uk

Description: Cruse Bereavement Scotland is a registered charity which offers free bereavement care and support to people who have experienced the loss of someone close. They have local offices and a website including details and support information.

Contact: Riverview House
              Friarton Road
              Perth
              PH2 8DF

              Tel: 01738 444 178

Disability Rights Commission

Website: www.drc-gb.org/scotland

Description: The Disability Rights Commission (DRC) is an independent organisation with the goal of 'a society where all disabled people can participate fully as equal citizens'. The DRC in Scotland are here to make sure that the DRC can deliver rights for disabled people in Scotland effectively and that Scottish issues influence the DRC' s work across Britain.

Contact: DRC Helpline
              Freepost / MID 02164
              Stratford upon Avon
              CV37 9BR

              Tel: 08457 622 633
              Textphone: 08457 622 644

Down's Syndrome Scotland

Website: www.dsscotland.org.uk

Description: Down's Syndrome Scotland works to improve the quality of life for everyone with Down's syndrome. Our members include people with Down's syndrome, families and professionals. We provide information, support and advice.

Contact: 158-160 Balgreen Road
Edinburgh
EH11 3AU

Tel: 0131 313 4225
Fax: 0131 313 4285
Email: info@dsscotland.org.uk

Dyslexia Scotland

Website: www.dyslexiascotland.org.uk

Description: Dyslexia Scotland aims to raise public awareness of dyslexia and its related difficulties, and offers advice and support for those with dyslexia.

Contact: Stirling Business Centre
Unit 3
Wellgreen
Stirling
FK8 2DZ

Tel: 01786 44 66 50
Fax: 01786 47 12 35
Helpline No. 08448 00 84 84 (lo-call rate)
Email: info@dyslexiascotland.org.uk

Dyspraxia Foundation

Website: www.dyspraxiafoundation.org.uk

Description: The Dyspraxia Foundation aims to support individuals and families affected by developmental dyspraxia and to increase understanding and awareness of dyspraxia. The Foundation also supports a network of local groups across the UK and organises conferences.

Contact: 8 West Alley
Hitchin
Herts SG5 1EG

Tel: 01462 455 052
Fax: 01462 455 052
Helpline: 01462 454 986 (Mon–Fri 10am–2pm)
Email: dyspraxia@dyspraxiafoundation.org.uk

Education Law Unit

Website: www.edlaw.org.uk

Description: Govan Law Centre's Education Law Unit is Scotland's expert legal resource in the field of school education, with a particular focus on the rights of disabled pupils and pupils with additional support needs. The Education Law Unit works in partnership with schools, education authorities, parents' groups and charities to make pupils' rights in education a reality.

Contact: Education Law Unit
Govan Law Centre
47 Burleigh Street
Govan
Glasgow G51 3LB

Tel: 0141 445 1955
Fax: 0141 445 3934
Email: advice@edlaw.org.uk

Enable Scotland

Website: www.enable.org.uk

Description: ENABLE Scotland is a dynamic charitable organisation run by its members. It campaigns for a better life for children and adults with learning disabilities and supports them and their families to participate, work and live in their local communities.

Contact: 6th Floor
7 Buchanan Street
Glasgow
G1 3HL

Tel: 0141 226 4541
Email: enable@enable.org.uk

Enquire

Website: www.enquire.org.uk

Description: Enquire is the national advice and information service for matters relating to additional support for learning.

Contact: Children in Scotland
5 Shandwick Place
Edinburgh
EH2 4RG

Tel: 0131 222 2425
Fax: 0131 228 9852
Helpline: 0845 123 2303
Typetalk: 0800 959 598
Email: info@enquire.org.uk

Epilepsy Scotland

Website: www.epilepsyscotland.org.uk

Description: Epilepsy Scotland aims to improve the quality of life for people with epilepsy and their families. They run a free confidential helpline.

Contact: 48 Govan Road
Glasgow
G51 1JL

Tel: 0141 427 4911
Fax: 0141 419 1709
Helpline: Freephone 0808 800 2 200
Email: enquiries@epilepsyscotland.org.uk

HM Inspectorate of Education (HMIe)

Website: www.scotland.gov.uk/hmie

Description: HMIe inspects and reviews Scottish primary and secondary schools, nursery education, further education colleges and local authority education departments.

Contact: Denholm House
Almondvale Business Park
Almondvale Way
Livingston
EH54 6GA

Tel: 01506 600 200

Home Education UK

Website: www.home-education.org.uk

Description: Home Education UK aims to provide support to people home educating or intending to home educate in the UK. They do this by providing online information and resources to home educators.

ISEA (Independent Special Education Advice) (Scotland)

Website: www.isea.org.uk

Description: ISEA provides information, advice and support, including advocacy / representation, to parents and carers of children with additional support needs.

Contact: 164 High Street
Dalkeith
Midlothian
EH22 1AY

Tel/Fax: 0131 454 0096 (D.E.C.I.D.E . Project)
Tel: 0131 454 0144 (Advocacy Project)
Email (D.E.C.I.D.E. Project): lofficer@isea.org.uk
Email (Advocacy Project): advocacy@isea.org.uk

Learning and Teaching Scotland

Website: www.ltscotland.org.uk

Description: Learning and Teaching Scotland offer consultancy to schools regarding curriculum development and produce publications on the curriculum and how to adapt it for pupils with special education needs.

Contact: 74 Victoria Crescent Road
Glasgow
G12 9JN

From January 2006 Learning and Teaching Scotland will be based at a new office at: The Optima

58 Robertson Street
Glasgow
G2 8JD

Tel: 0141 337 5000
Fax: 0141 337 5050
Email: enquiries@LTScotland.org.uk

The National Autistic Society Scotland

Website: www.autism.org.uk

Description: The National Autistic Society exists to champion the rights and interests of all people with autism and to ensure that they and their families receive quality services appropriate to their needs. The website includes information about autism and Asperger syndrome, the NAS and its services and activities.

Contact: Central Chambers
First Floor, 109 Hope Street
Glasgow G2 6LL

Tel: 0141 221 8090
Fax: 0141 221 8118
Email: scotland@nas.org.uk

National Deaf Children's Society Scotland

Website: www.ndcs.org.uk/ndcs_networks/scotland/index.html

Description: The National Deaf Children's Society (NCDS) is the only UK charity solely dedicated to the support of all deaf children and young people, their families and professionals working with them. We do this by offering clear balanced information and support to families advocating for deaf children, young people and their families providing opportunities for young deaf people to develop social skills, confidence and independence working with professionals and policy makers to ensure high quality services are available for all campaigning and lobbying on behalf of deaf children, young people and their families.

Contact: 187-189 Central Chambers
93 Hope Street
Glasgow G2 6LD

Tel: 0141 248 4457
Fax: 0141 248 2597
Minicom: 0141 222 4476
Email: ndcs.scotland@ndcs.org.uk

Parentline Scotland

Website: www.children1st.org.uk/parentline

Description: At some time all parents find that parenting can be difficult, stressful, even impossible. ParentLine Scotland is the free, confidential, telephone helpline for parents and anyone caring for a child in Scotland. You can call about any problem, however big or small.

Contact: C/O Children 1st
83 Whitehouse Loan
Edinburgh EH9 1AT

Tel: 0131 446 2333 Fax: 0131 446 2339
Helpline: 0808 800 2222

Parentzone

Website: www.parentzonescotland.gov.uk

Description: Parentzone helps parents to get involved in their children's education by providing the latest information on education in Scotland, offering advice to parents on how to support their children's learning, providing facts about individual schools, up-to-date news and publications and links to useful organisations.

Contacts: You can e-mail via the website.

The Royal National Institute of the Blind

Website: www.rnib.org.uk

Description: The RNIB offers practical support and advice to blind people and those with visual impairments.

Contact: Dunedin House
25 Ravelston Terrace
Edinburgh
EH4 3TP

Tel: 0131 311 8500
Fax: 0131 311 8529
Email: rnibscotland@rnib.org.uk

RNID for Deaf and Hard of Hearing People (Scotland)

Website: www.rnid.org.uk

Description: RNID in Scotland represents the 758,000 deaf and hard of hearing people who live in the country, as well as their families and others who work with them or for their benefit. Our staff and volunteers offer a wide range of services, including communication, information, care and employment services. We campaign in many areas and act to raise awareness of deafness in Scotland.

Contact: Crowngate Business Centre
Brook Street
Glasgow
G40 3AP

Tel: 0141 554 0053
Helpline: 0808 808 0123 (Freephone)
Textphone: 0808 808 9000 (Freephone)
Email: rnidscotland@rnid.org.uk

Schoolhouse Home Education Association

Website: www.schoolhouse.org.uk

Description: Schoolhouse offers information and support to parents/carers throughout Scotland who seek to take personal responsibility for the education of their children, families who have chosen, or are contemplating home-based education, and those who wish to safeguard the right of families to educate in accordance with their own philosophy and with due regard to the wishes and feelings of their children.

Contact: PO BOX 18044
            Glenrothes
            KY7 9AD

            Tel: 0870 745 0968
            Email: info@schoolhouse.org.uk

Scottish Anti-Bullying Network

Website: www.antibullying.net

Description: The Scottish Executive established the Network in 1999 so that teachers, parents and young people could share ideas about how bullying should be tackled. In the final months before the ABN is replaced by a new anti-bullying service for Scotland in April 2006 we shall be concentrating on helping those adults who work in and with school communities to develop better approaches to tackling bullying.

Contact: Anti-Bullying Network
            Moray House Schools of Education
            University of Edinburgh
            Holyrood Road
            Edinburgh
            EH8 8AQ

Scottish Child Law Centre

Website: www.sclc.org.uk

Description: The Scottish Child Law Centre is an independent charitable organisation, based in Edinburgh, which provides services to the whole of Scotland. The aim of the centre is to promote knowledge and use of Scots law and children's rights for the benefit of children and young people in Scotland. The SCLC provides a free telephone advice service on all aspects of Scots law relating to children and young people, as well as producing a range of publications and providing training.

Contact: 54 East Crosscauseway
Edinburgh
EH8 9HD

Tel: 0131 667 6333 Fax: 0131 662 1713
Helpline for under 18s: 0800 328 8970
Email: enquiries@sclc.org.uk

Scottish Committee of the Council of Tribunals

Website: www.council-on-tribunals.gov.uk

Description: The Council on Tribunals and its Scottish Committee are independent bodies first established in 1958. The Council on Tribunals supervises the constitution and working of tribunals and inquiries in England, Scotland and Wales, seeking to ensure they are open, fair and impartial.

Contact: 44 Palmerston Place
Edinburgh
EH12 5BJ

Tel: 0131 220 1236
Fax: 0131 225 4271
Email: sccot@gtnet.gov.uk

Scottish Executive Education Department

Website: www.scotland.gov.uk

Description: The Executive wants to ensure that everybody has access to learning opportunities that can help them achieve their full potential - giving children and young people the best possible start in life as they move from school to university and college or into the workforce, ensuring employability and adaptability throughout life. There is a specific division that deals with Additional Support Needs within the Scottish Executive Education Department.

Contact: Victoria Quay, Edinburgh EH6 6QQ

For general education enquiries contact:
Tel: 0131 556 8400

For the Additional Support Needs Division contact:
Tel: 0131 244 4914
Fax: 0131 244 7943
Email: ASLAct@scotland.gsi.gov.uk

Scottish Human Rights Centre

Website: www.scottishhumanrightscentre.org.uk

Description: The Scottish Human Rights Centre is a non-governmental organisation which aims to promote human rights in Scotland. SHRC provides a free advice and information service which is open to the public and can answer queries on education and other human rights issues.

Contact: 146 Holland Street
Glasgow
G2 4NG

Tel: 0141 332 5960
Fax: 0141 332 5309
Email: info@scottishhumanrightscentre.org.uk

Scottish Mediation Network

Website: www.scottishmediation.org.uk

Description: The Scottish Mediation Network aim to put mediation into the mainstream, widely available and clearly understood as a first option for resolving disputes of all kinds in Scotland.

Contact: 18 York Place
Edinburgh
EH1 3EP

Tel: 0131 556 1221
Email: info@scottishmediation.org.uk

Scottish Network for Able Pupils

Website: www.ablepupils.com

Description: The Scottish Network for Able Pupils (SNAP) was established in 1995. Since its inception SNAP has offered support and advice to the Scottish Education system in three main areas: publications, staff development and national conferences.

Contact: Room 556
University of Glasgow
11 Eldon Street
Glasgow
G3 6NH

Tel: 0141 330 3071
Fax: 0141 330 5451
Email: snap@educ.gla.ac.uk

Scottish Parent Teacher Council

Website: www.sptc.info

Description: The SPTC's aim is to advance education by encouraging the fullest co-operation between home and school, education authorities, central government and all those concerned with education in Scotland.

Contact: 53 George Street
             Edinburgh
             EH2 2HT

             Tel: 0131 226 4378
             Fax: 0870 706 5814
             Email: sptc@sptc.info

Scottish Public Services Ombudsman

Website: www.scottishombudsman.org.uk

Description: The Scottish Public Services Ombudsman provides an open, accountable and accessible public services complaints system.

Contact: 4 Melville Street
             Edinburgh
             EH3 7NS

             Tel: 0870 011 5378
             Fax: 0870 011 5379
             Email: enquiries@scottishombudsman.org.uk

Scottish Refugee Council

Website: www.scottishrefugeecouncil.org.uk

Description: Scottish Refugee Council is an independent charity dedicated to providing advice, information and assistance to asylum seekers and refugees living in Scotland. We also provide specialist services in areas such as housing and welfare, education and employment, family reunion, women's issues, community development, the media and the arts.

Contact: 5 Cadogan Square
Glasgow
G2 7PH

Tel: 0141 248 9799
Fax: 01471 243 2499
Email: info@scottishrefugeecouncil.org.uk

Scottish School Boards Association

Website: www.schoolboard-scotland.com

Description: SSBA represents the interests of all Scottish School Boards. The SSBA Executive Membership is elected from every Education Authority across Scotland. SSBA delivers training to Scottish School Boards and offers help and advice to individuals and School Boards. The Scottish School Board Association gives focus and voice to the opinion of Scottish School Boards representing 1.25 million parents.

Contact: Newall Terrace
Dumfries
DG1 1LW

Telephone/Fax : 01387 260428
Email: ssba@schoolboard-scotland.com

Scottish Society for Autism Headquarters

Website: www.autism-in-scotland.org.uk

Description: The Scottish Society for Autism is a Scottish registered charity established in 1968 and works together with persons with Autism Spectrum Disorder (ASD), their families, carers, and other organisations, agencies, and individuals in Scotland to provide and promote exemplary services and training in education, care, support and life opportunities for persons of all ages with ASD, influence policy and practice to ensure the best possible education, care, support and life opportunities for persons of all ages with ASD, and raise public awareness about what ASD is, and how it affects the lives of individuals and families in Scotland.

Contact: New Struan School
              A Centre for Autism
              Bradbury Campus
              100 Smithfield Loan
              Alloa
              FK10 1NP

              Tel: 01259 300 9281 or 01259 222 000
              Fax: 01259 724 239
              Email: newstruan@autism-in-scotland.org.uk

Scottish Traveller Education Programme

Website: www.scottishtravellered.net

Description: STEP is based at Edinburgh University and is funded by the Scottish Executive Education Department. Its remit is to develop, promote and support inclusive educational approaches for Gypsies and Travellers. STEP listens to and represents the views of Gypsy and Traveller children, young people and parents about education, and encourages respect for their cultural traditions and current circumstances. It works with teachers and other professionals to promote the development of practices which support diversity and address racism, harassment and bullying. STEP encourages inter-agency working, which acknowledges the links between education, housing, health and other key social services.

Contact: The University of Edinburgh
2.5 Charteris Land
Holyrood Road
Edinburgh
EH8 8AQ

Tel: 0131 651 6444
Fax: 0131 651 6511
Email: step@education.ed.ac.uk

See Me Scotland

Website: www.seemescotland.org

Description: The 'see me' campaign was launched in October 2002 to challenge stigma and discrimination around mental ill-health in Scotland. 'see me' is unable to give direct advice and support to people with mental health problems and those experiencing stigma/discrimination but their website does have useful resources and factsheets.

Contact: 9-13 Maritime Street
              Edinburgh EH6 6SB

              Tel:0131 624 8945
              Fax: 0131 624 8901
              Email: info@seemescotland.org

Sense Scotland

Website: www.sensescotland.org.uk

Description: Sense Scotland is a leader in the field of communication and innovative support services for people who are marginalised because of challenging behaviour, health care issues and the complexity of their support needs. It is a significant provider of services and also engages in policy development for children and adults with complex support needs because of deafblindness or sensory impairment, learning disability or physical disability.

Contact: 43 Middlesex Street
              Kinning Park
              Glasgow G41 1EE

              Tel: 0141 429 0294
              Fax: 0141 429 0295
              Text: 0141 418 7170
              Email: info@sensescotland.org.uk

Skill Scotland

Website: www.skill.org.uk

Description: Skill Scotland operates an information and advice service, provides volunteering opportunities, informs and influences key decision makers, runs conferences and works with its members.

Contact: National Bureau for Students with Disabilities
Norton Park
57 Albion Road
Edinburgh
EH7 5QY

Tel: 0131 475 2348
Fax: 0131 475 2397
Freephone/Text: 0800 328 5050
(Mon-Thur 1.30-4.30p.m.)
Email: admin@skillscotland.org.uk

U.K. Information Commissioner

Website: www.dataprotection.gov.uk

Description: The Commissioner is a UK independent supervisory authority reporting directly to the UK Parliament and has an international role as well as a national one.

Contact: Information Commissioner
             Wycliffe House
             Water Lane
             Wilmslow
             Cheshire
             SK9 5AF

             Tel: 01625 545 700
             Fax: 01625 524 510

Who Cares? Scotland

Website: www.whocaresscotland.org

Description: Who Cares? Scotland is an independent organisation, which is not part of social work and which provides advocacy and support for young people in care.

Contact: Oswald Chambers
             5 Oswald Street
             Glasgow
             G1 4QR

             Tel: 0141 226 6441
             Email: enquiries@whocaresscotland.org

7.7 Resources for your child

If your child is experiencing a difficult situation it is important that they are able to find information that they find helpful, supportive and accessible. We have listed a range of resources, mainly online, that your child might find useful. Many of the organisations listed in section 7.6 (contacts) also provide information and support for children and young people.

www.enquire.org.uk/youngpeople

Enquire is the Scottish advice and information service for additional support for learning.

Enquire guides for young people

What are additional support needs? – an introductory guide

Going to secondary school – a guide for primary 7 pupils who will be going to mainstream secondary school

Have your say – A film about young people joining in and getting their views across at secondary school (comes with British Sign Language and teacher's notes)

What's the plan? – a guide to the ways in which young people can be involved in planning their education

People who can help – a guide to the roles of professionals in and outside school who can support young people

Round the table – a guide to going to meetings

---

www.youngscot.org.uk

Website with a wide range of information for children and young people.

www.thesite.org.uk

Has information on all kinds of issues affecting children and young people and includes the 'local advice finder' where you can search for a range of services in your area.

www.support4learning.org.uk/community/students.htm

A portal site with links to many children and young people's websites, particularly ones relating to further or higher education.

www.justlikeyou.org

Children and young people's website produced by the 'see me' campaign that aims to challenge stigma and discrimination around mental ill health.

www.article12.org

An organisation led by young people to promote children's and young people's rights under the United Nations Convention on the Rights of the Child (section 1.7 of this handbook for more on your child's rights).

www.lgbtyouth.org.uk

Information and advice for lesbian, gay, bisexual and transgender young people.

www.bullying.co.uk

Website with advice for children and young people and their parents. This site includes legal advice which applies to England and Wales and may be different in Scotland, we have included it because some of the more general advice may be useful.

www.childrens-hearings.co.uk/infochildren

Children and young people's website explaining the Children's Hearings System.

www.youngcarers.net

Support for children and young people who are involved in helping to care for someone.

www.befriending.co.uk

Information about befriending including contacts for befriending projects around Scotland.

Index

Note: bold page numbers indicate definitions and major references

reading difficulties 18, 28
reading lists 134-7, 140-5
Record of Needs 5, 15-16, 17, 115
reference, making see under
  Additional Support Needs
  Tribunals
references and sources 2, 110-72
  contacts and websites 146-70
  glossary 110-17
  information on factors leading to
  additional support needs 117-25
  professionals 128-34
  reading list 134-7, 140-5
  resources for your child 171-2
  specific conditions 125-8
Refugee Council, Scottish 165
requests for school places see placing
  requests
Resolve: ASL mediation service iv
resources for your child 171-2
responsibilities, major 9-10
restraint/physical intervention 106-7
reviews of CSPs 44, 45, 68, 115
Riddell, S. 144
Riddell Report (1999) 5
rights
  to basic information 66, 67
  child's involvement 74-6
  legal right to be involved 73
  major 8-9, 10
  right to know 69-70
  support or advocacy 77-8
  UN Convention of Rights of
  Child 5, 11, 172
  see also Disability Rights
  Commission; Human Rights;
  mediation
RNID for Deaf and Hard of
  Hearing People (Scotland) 159
Royal National Institute of Blind 159
Rubella (German measles) 127
safety 107
Salamanca Statement (UNESCO) 5
Same as you? report 6

school 9, 10, 115, 116
  abroad 57
  age 115
  development plan 74
  education, benefit from 13
  education defined 12
  grant-aided 113
  holidays and support 107-8
  independent/grant-aided 55, 56-7,
  79, 113
  information, right to 66
  mainstream 114
  nurse 133
  requests for place see placing
  requests
  special 55, 56, 116
  support from outwith 28-31
  support from within 27-8
  working in partnership with 64-6
  see also stages of schooling;
  teachers; transitions and under
  plans
Schoolhouse Home Education
  Association 62, 160
Scottish Anti-Bullying Network 160
Scottish Child Law Centre 161
Scottish Committee of Council on
  Tribunals 84, 88, 161
Scottish Consumer Council ii, iv, 3,
  67, 70
  on education law 144-5
Scottish Executive 115
  Assessing our children's educational
  needs 5
  Beattie Report (1999) 5-6
  dispute resolution 83
  Education Department 4, 162
  home education guidance 62
  Inclusive schooling 142
  information access 72
  Integrated Assessment Framework
  46
  Ministers 91, 94
  race equality 142, 144

About the Scottish Consumer Council

The Scottish Consumer Council (SCC) is a non-departmental public body, set up by government in 1975. Our purpose is to make all consumers matter. We do this by putting forward the consumer interest, particularly that of disadvantaged groups within society, by researching, campaigning and working with those who can make a difference to achieve beneficial change.

Over almost 30 years, we have taken an active role in education policy, conducting research and working closely with other bodies and government agencies to ensure that the voice of parents (and more recently children and young people) as consumers of education is heard.

About Children in Scotland

Children in Scotland is Scotland's national organisation for organisations and professionals working with and for children, young people and their families. It exists to identify and promote the interests of children, young people and their families and to ensure that policies, services and other provisions are of the highest possible quality and are able to meet the needs of a diverse society.

Children in Scotland has particular expertise in additional support for learning including facilitating the involvement of parents in the development of the Education (Additional Support for Learning) (Scotland) Act. The agency manages Enquire (the Scottish advice and information service for additional support for learning), runs the Resolve: ASL independent mediation service as well as advocacy services in Stirling, Aberdeenshire and Moray, and has recently developed the Additional Support for Learning Network.

as an authoritative statement on the law, which only the courts can rule on, we believe it will be a valuable source for parents of children and young people who have additional support needs.

Graeme Millar

Chairman,
Scottish Consumer Council

Bronwen Cohen

Chief Executive,
Children in Scotland